Pro Tools
Surround Sound Mixing

Pro Tools
Surround Sound Mixing

by Rich Tozzoli

Backbeat
Books
San Francisco

Published by Backbeat Books
600 Harrison Street, San Francisco, CA 94107
www.backbeatbooks.com
email: books@musicplayer.com

CMP
United Business Media

An imprint of CMP Information
Publishers of *Guitar Player*, *Bass Player*,
Keyboard, and *EQ* magazines

Digidesign and Pro Tools are trademarks of Digidesign, a division of Avid
Technology, and names and logos are used with permission.

Distributed to the book trade in the US and Canada by
Publishers Group West, 1700 Fourth Street, Berkeley, CA 94710

Distributed to the music trade in the US and Canada by
Hal Leonard Publishing, P.O. Box 13819, Milwaukee, WI 53213

Interior design and composition: Leigh McLellan
Cover design: Patrick Devine
Editors: George Madaraz and Karl Coryat

Library of Congress Cataloging-in-Publication Data

Tozzoli, Rich.
  Pro Tools surround sound mixing / by Rich Tozzoli.
     p. cm.
  Includes bibliographical references and index.
  ISBN 0-87930-832-X (alk. paper)
  1. Pro Tools. 2. Digital audio editors. 3. Surround-sound systems. I. Title.

  ML74.4.P76T39 2005
  621.389'3'0285536--dc22
                                    2005002693

Printed in the United States of America

05 06 07 08   5 4 3 2 1

ISBN: 0-87930-832-X

Contents

Appendix A
Follow the DVD   147

Appendix B
Additional Resources   157

Index   159

Introduction

Producing and mixing surround sound with Pro Tools is exciting, challenging, and infinitely rewarding. Like anything else worthwhile, it's a skill developed through trial and error, learning from others, practice, and making mistakes—lots of them. My goal in writing this book is to pass on what I learned by making those mistakes, and to help you with all the little tips and tricks you can discover by "doing." Having completed over 25 surround music mixing projects for DVD, SA-CD, and HDTV formats, I can follow my own growth and progression by simply listening back to each one. Of course, they were all done using Pro Tools.

When speaking to a group at a surround seminar or in class, one of the first things I tell them is that there are no rules when it comes to multichannel production. Yes, there are basic principles to be followed (which I'll explain in this book), but the rest is up to your imagination. When you finish your first surround mix and play it back for your client or band members, chances are good you'll have just blown their minds. I've experienced this many times, and whether it's a multi-platinum star or an unsigned local artist, their excitement level is always the same. It's a feeling I hope you'll all soon experience.

Digidesign's Pro Tools is an amazingly powerful platform to create surround with. Having said that, this book is aimed at helping those with a prior basic working knowledge of Pro Tools reach that next level of production. Like most other functions within the Pro Tools platform, there is usually more than one way to accomplish each task. The techniques I have outlined in this book will hopefully provide you a starting point to discover your own methods of working.

I strongly believe that having even a fundamental comprehension of multi-channel sound will put you ahead of your competition. Whether it's for music, film, post-production, or games, the future shines a little brighter for those who understand the concepts of surround sound—especially when using Pro Tools.

Getting Started

Surround Sound in the Movies Started with Walt Disney's *Fantasia*

Walt Disney was a true innovator and pioneer in multichannel production. Even though hundreds of years earlier composers had written symphonies placing musicians throughout the concert hall, it was Disney who created the first surround film experience with his 1938 epic, *Fantasia*. Using a technology aptly called Fantasound, they treated audiences to a new experience: The mix radiated from a front left, front right, and front center speaker. Behind the audience were "house" left, "house" center, and "house" right speakers, derived from the front left and right channels. Does that setup sound familiar?

The production of *Fantasia* had several other innovations we still use to this day. Disney engineer William Garity designed a three-way circuit to help mix the film, called "The Panpot." It basically created "motion" in the sound by altering levels between speakers, printing audio across several recorders mechanically synchronized to each other. On top of that, *Fantasia* engineer John Volkman used eight recorders to capture the orchestra, including one for a room microphone and one for the overall mix. Multitrack recording and overdubbing had been born.

How We Got to Where We Are Today: From Mono to Multichannel

Think about when you're looking through collections of old LPs and you see those *Featuring Stereophonic Sound* labels on the top of the album covers. Considering that Bell Labs was experimenting with three-channel stereo sound way back in the 1930s, it took quite a while for stereo to evolve beyond mono. It also makes you realize how advanced Disney was with his surround playback system, before it was literally sunk at sea while on its way to a demonstration in Russia!

Filmmakers had always taken a slightly more sophisticated approach to sound, since many felt that stereo playback alone did not convey an epic experience inside a movie theater. Many differing formats and experimental methods were tried. To remain practical for both synchronization and widespread distribution, matrix encoding (the delivery of multiple channels on stereo tracks) became common, such as Dolby Stereo (first introduced in 1976). This format was developed for 35mm prints, using optical technology to carry front Left, Center, and Right channels, as well as a single mono rear surround signal. To this day, prints with digital soundtracks also carry an analog Dolby Stereo track for compatibility purposes.

There were, however, a number of discrete systems developed during the 1950s that recorded the audio directly onto a magnetic strip on the film itself. Formats such as Cinemascope, Panavision, Warnerphonic, and even something called Todd AO (which had printed surround sound on a 70mm piece of film) were developed. They all were ultimately abandoned due to high cost, overall incompatibility, or simply an inability to compete with advancing technologies.

As theatrical sound kept evolving, and as six-track multichannel audio became more common, Dolby Digital and DTS slowly became the standards for 5.1 delivery. There are other film formats, such as IMAX or SDDS (a 35mm optically encoded 7.1 format with left front, mid-left front, center, mid-right front, right front, left and right surrounds, and an LFE), but the typical 5.1 format still reigns supreme.

Paralleling the progress of film sound were the advances in home audio playback. Aside from the failed Quad format (a technology ahead of its time), the VHS revolution brought about a growing interest in playing back movies in the comfort of one's own home. Suddenly, there were more formats being thrown at the consumer: Laser Discs, cassettes, CDs, stereo television broadcasts, laser discs, and decent portable players became the norm. Also, the development of Dolby Pro Logic meant a surround experience with four channels (Left, Center, Right, and Surround, generally known as "LCRS") could be had in the consumer's living room, with decoding through one's receiver. Multichannel home theater now had its seeds firmly planted.

Eventually, the boundaries between cinema, music, and television broadcast blurred within each other. With the massive acceptance of the DVD format and a common 5.1 standard firmly in place, surround sound delivery is now commonplace. The consumer home theater market has exploded, and a quick glance through any electronics store circular will show dozens of 5.1 multichannel systems for sale. Add to that surround delivery through satellite and cable television, in video games, and even over the Internet, and you have yourself a serious market to work with!

What Does the Term "5.1" Mean?

This is certainly one of the most common terms thrown about when describing surround sound, but it can be misleading. In some ways, it's almost like calling all tissues "Kleenexes." The term "5.1" derives from having six discrete channels of surround sound: Front Left, Center, Front Right, Left Surround, Right Surround, and LFE (Low Frequency Effects), or the .1 channel.

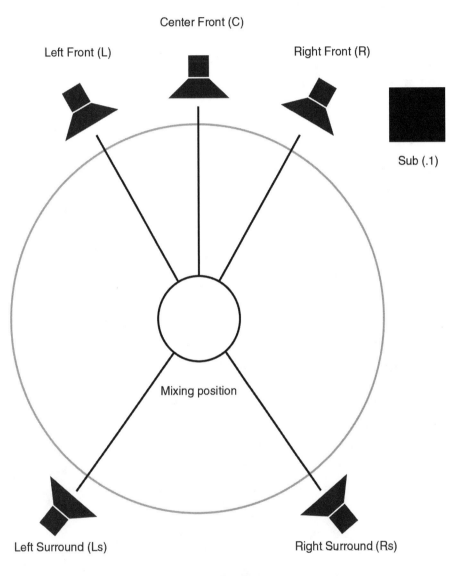

Fig. 1-1: 5.1 diagram

It's important to understand that discrete and matrixed surround are not the same thing. Matrixed surround, such as Dolby Pro Logic and Pro Logic II, is printed on stereo analog tracks and decoded by the receiver. The Center and surround signals (mono surround in Pro Logic) are recovered from the stereo source and steered to the appropriate speakers. When you're watching a movie on a VHS tape and listening to it in surround, that's what you're listening to: a matrixed signal. In contrast, when you watch a DVD with a Dolby Digital or DTS track, or listen to a multichannel (more than two channels) DVD-Audio or SA-CD disc, that's discrete surround. As for the choice of what to mix, discrete surround is generally the preferred way to go, since it offers the highest quality. However, matrixed surround sound certainly has its applications as well. Read on!

For explanations of additional surround formats, see Chapter 10, Current Surround Formats.

Music in Surround: The Focus of This Book

My specialty is the recording, mixing, and production of music in surround sound. Therefore, most of the information and examples in this book will relate to that subject. However, as you all know, multichannel production encompasses many areas, including television commercials, motion pictures, sporting and Internet broadcasts, and video games. In order to expand the subject and try to provide you more knowledge, I have included extra subchapters and additional interviews with professionals outside of my field. Also provided is information on many products that can help you record, mix, and produce multichannel audio.

I feel that the overall concept of surround sound applies "across the board." Once you understand the general principles, you can narrow in on the specifics of each area, as needed.

Which Pro Tools Systems Can Mix in Surround?

Currently, Pro Tools HD, HD Accel, and Mix systems operating version 5.1 software or higher support full multichannel mixing.

In addition to this book, I highly recommend reading *The Pro Tools Reference Guide*. There are several chapters that deal specifically with surround sound and which are full of valuable information. I've also included a supplementary list of recommended titles at the end of this book.

CHAPTER 2

Monitoring in Surround

Speakers and Setup

Setting up your speakers to monitor in surround sound is not as difficult as it may seem, though there are several issues that need careful attention. As with stereo, the focus should be on the accurate, balanced representation of your audio elements.

The overall objective of your surround mix is to create an exciting sonic experience that takes you outside of stereo—but it is an experience that you want to share with consumers in their homes. It is therefore important to *think like a consumer but mix like a professional*. This means taking steps to create as "tuned" a mixing environment as is physically and financially possible. It's vital to minimize room reflections, especially early ones, so that your mix sounds good outside your room. Take time and effort to ensure that the low end in your room is as correct as possible, even if you have to buy bass traps or diffusers in order to help minimize standing waves. There are some great-sounding and relatively inexpensive options available for treating spaces—just check the pages of your favorite professional audio magazine. If you're working on a really tight budget, you can always make up your own room treatments by doing a little research online. Another small but important issue is to try to minimize background noise—your computer fans, outboard gear, drives, etc.

Once you've done your best to make the room itself sound good (and quiet), you can set up your speakers. Most professionals suggest mixing surround with a matched set of direct-firing (not dipole) full-range speakers, with at least one subwoofer. The reason direct-firing speakers are highly recommended is they minimize reflections—something you need to avoid as much as possible when mixing. I happen to use five self-powered mid-field monitors ("self-powered" means they have their own amplifiers), along with a subwoofer from the same company, made specifically for those speakers. I prefer using mid-field speakers for surround because I find that they are very similar to consumer speakers, yet they still allow me to mix with fine detail. Many companies make excellent complete 5.1 surround speaker setups at very reasonable prices these days, so there is no excuse not to have a decent setup. It's an important part of your investment into mixing surround.

Speaker Placement

As with stereo, you should try to set up your speakers to create a "sweet spot." I'm sure at one time or another you've all slid your chair back and forth with your eyes closed to try to find it. It's important to realize that this is for setup only! When you mix, you should not rely on that sweet spot alone; instead, you should try to mix for the entire room. Sometimes I'll even turn to one side and mix, just to hear the overall sound from another angle.

Ideally, the surround mix position should have the signal from all five (or more) speakers arriving at the same time. I achieve this equidistant setup in my room quite simply—by having each of the speakers placed literally at the same distance from where I sit. I happen to use the old-fashioned method: a piece of string that gets stretched out to each tweeter. Of course, you could use any method that gets the job done accurately—from tape measures to lasers.

Since the speakers I use are mid-fields on lightweight stands, it's not a problem to move them around to make the sweet spot happen. If that's not possible in your room, then delays can be used to compensate. This is one of the features offered by the Waves 360 Manager plug-in for Pro Tools (see Chapter 9). It's important to note that if the sound of the all the speakers doesn't arrive at the mix position at the same time, comb filtering and phase issues may occur, therefore providing false results in your mix, so take the time to do this right; it will pay off later.

As for height requirements, there are several schools of thought. I happen to have the front three speakers (Left, Center, Right) at the same height, about where the tweeter of each meets my eyes and ears (almost four feet). My Left Rear and Right Rear speakers are about four inches higher, but angled slightly downward. However, you could have all the speakers at the same height if you choose. I prefer the slightly higher rear speakers because I have found that many consumers listen that way at home. It's up to you; there is no right or wrong setup. Just research what others do!

Other important placement issues include the angle at which the speakers face inward and how they are positioned in the overall surround field. Remember, surround sound was originally developed for cinema—and with that comes suggested home theater speaker placement to achieve cinematic sound. However, with the growing popularity of multichannel music, the placement of surround speakers

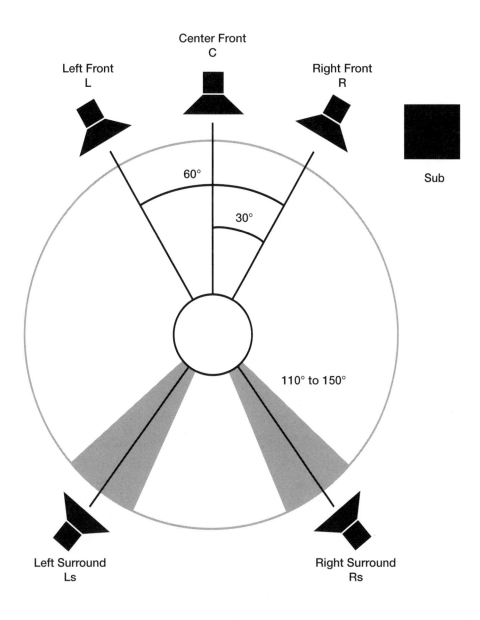

Left Front
L

Center Front
C

Right Front
R

Sub

60°

30°

110° to 150°

Left Surround
Ls

Right Surround
Rs

Fig. 2-1: Equal speaker distance for 5.1 setup

(especially the rears) to reproduce music properly may differ from room to room. Wow, more confusion!

Think about it: The nature of home theater playback for films is to include mostly ambience and effects in the surrounds, sometimes even using dipole speakers to fire the sound off in an array. The nature of audio can be anything in those channels: lots of audience mics for live concerts, direct sounds on studio releases, delays, vocals, guitars, effects, and whatever. Those same dipoles that sound great for cinema may not work for music. Certainly, music is a totally different animal. The key is to try to find a happy medium. (Hey, nobody said this would be *easy*, did they?)

The Front Speakers

The three front speakers—Left, Center, and Right—should ideally be placed the same distance from the mix position, with the front Left and Right forming an equilateral triangle.

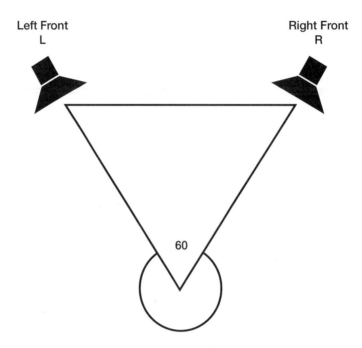

Fig. 2-2: Front L, C, R forming equilateral triangle

The Left and Right speakers should be angled in at about 30 degrees. However, steeper angles may be used; I myself prefer an angle of about 35 degrees. This is due to my room acoustics, the speaker design, and also because I feel that the 35-degree angle provides excellent compatibility for stereo monitoring.

The Center speaker should be directly in front, facing the mixer. Note that since all speakers should be the same distance from the mixer, it will therefore be positioned slightly back from the front Left/Right speakers, on an "arc."

Since most of us have video monitors directly in front of the mix position, you may have to place the center speaker above or below it (I have to lay mine on its side). If that is necessary, you should at least try to get the tweeters in a straight line in order to avoid any alignment problems. If necessary, you might even turn the speaker upside down in order to have that tweeter at the same height as the Left and Right Front speakers. As usual, experimentation is key.

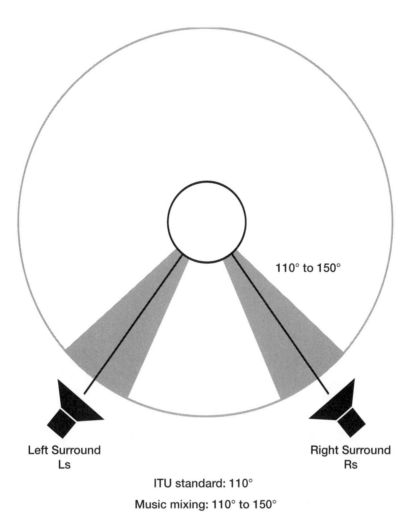

110° to 150°

Left Surround
Ls

Right Surround
Rs

ITU standard: 110°

Music mixing: 110° to 150°

Fig. 2-3: 2-3 rear speaker positioning

The Rear Speakers

The Rear Left and Right speakers (sometimes referred to as the "surround" speakers) should be toed inwards to the center of the mix position, at an angle between
110 and 150 degrees. I actually set mine right in the middle of that figure, angled
in at 130 degrees. This strikes a balance between a cinematic approach to home
theater and one that is specific to the enjoyment of music only.

The Subwoofer

Just as every room will be different, so too will the physical placement of the subwoofer vary. Most professionals place the subwoofer between the Left and Right
speakers, in front of the mix position. It's important to walk around your room and
listen for any standing waves. If you hear them, change the angle of your sub or its
physical position. It's also important to play some music that you are familiar with

through your system, and then do some additional placement using your ears. Sometimes that's the quickest and most efficient method. Just make sure you can't hear the direction the low frequencies are coming from. If you can, try either changing the angle or moving it away from a wall, or physically move the sub to another location.

The ITU Standard

Back in 1994, the ITU (International Telecommunications Union) released their recommendations for loudspeaker placement in a multichannel audio system. As we've already discussed, they agree that the Front Left and Right speakers should be angled inwards at 30 degrees, that the Center speaker face the mixer directly, and that all speakers be equidistant to the center spot. But they also suggest that the surround speakers be angled at 110 degrees, positioned almost to the side of the mixer. Now, that's fine for film applications, but not so great for music. Some music mixers I know don't follow the ITU standard exactly, primarily due to the fact that it was created for broadcast monitoring. Again, experiment with different setups to find what works best for your specific needs.

Calibration within Pro Tools

Calibrating your Pro Tools system before you calibrate your speakers is essential. If you don't take this step first, you may be aligning your speakers to a setup that doesn't sound right to begin with—and with five or more speakers to consider, you'd really be in trouble. Please take the time to do this right; it's worth it. Note that these same instructions can be found online or in your Pro Tools setup guides.

Calibration steps for a 192 or an 888 I/O:

1. First, create a new session with a mono track in Pro Tools. Open the Signal Generator plug-in and assign the output to the first mono out, with the fader set to unity gain.

2. On the Signal Generator plug-in (RTAS), select Sine Wave, then set the frequency to 1000Hz.

3. Adjust the LEVEL on the plug-in to –18dB, by simply typing in the value. (–18dB is a typical reference standard output level for a 192 or 888 I/O interface.)

4. Take an AC voltmeter and measure across pins 2 & 3 of the XLR output, or across the tip and ring of a connected TRS cable. The voltage on the voltmeter has to read 1.228V for a +4dBu system or .316V for –10dBV, so adjust your outputs on the I/O interface accordingly.

5. Go through your channel outputs one at a time. You can either create new channels with plug-ins or just move the I/O Output over, one channel at a time.

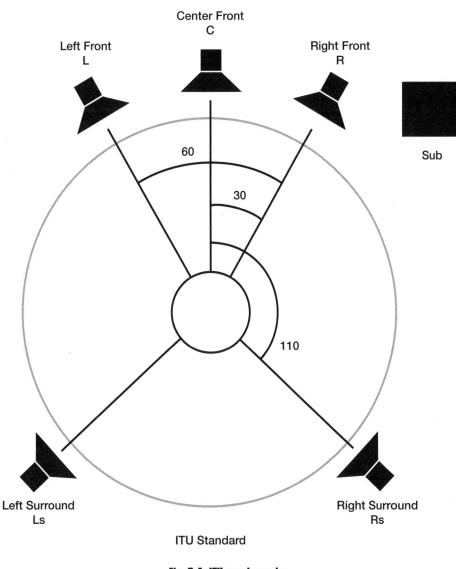

Left Front
L

Center Front
C

Right Front
R

60

30

110

Sub

Left Surround
Ls

Right Surround
Rs

ITU Standard

Fig. 2-4: ITU speaker setup

6. Once you have all the outputs adjusted correctly, you can do the inputs.

Create an additional audio channel if you need to, and route the output of that channel to the first channel's input. Then create a mono aux input with its fader set to unity. On the aux channel, assign the input to the first mono input and the output to the first mono output.

1. Measure the voltage across the first output. Adjust the trim of the first input so the meter reads 1.228V for +4dBu or .316V for −10dBV.

2. Connect the last output to the next input, changing the input of the aux track as you move from channel to channel. One you've adjusted the levels, you're ready to rock.

Save the session as "Pro Tools Calibration" for next time!

Speaker and Room Calibrations

The next step in the process of tuning your room is to calibrate the studio itself. For Pro Tools users, I highly suggest using the Waves M360 Manager and LFE Filter plug-ins (see Chapter 9). This will allow you to not only calibrate your speakers directly from your Pro Tools setup, but also save the settings as a preset to be called up at any time afterwards.

Note that there are also some great calibration discs available, such as *How to Set Up Your Surround Studio DVD* by Bobby Owsinski, or Tomlinson Holman's *TMH Digital Audio Test and Measurement Discs*. These can help ensure your system plays back at balanced levels.

To open the Digidesign calibration session, go to your Pro Tools Folder > Pro Tools Utilities > Calibration Mode Templates > MIX IO Calibrations Templates> Calibration Template (8 ch.). This will provide you with a 1kHz Sine wave at –18dB, across the first eight channels of your interface. Using an SPL meter set for C-weighting on SLOW scale, select Pink Noise on the Signal Generator and individually calibrate your monitors for equal playback at your desired listening level. Also, since monitor systems and controllers vary widely, you may need to refer to the speaker calibration directions given by the manufacturer.

When calibrating with the Waves M360 as explained below, you will be using 5.1 tracks and faders. These are just like your usual mono or stereo tracks, but they carry multiple channels of audio. When you're ready to mix surround, you will also be changing your Pro Tools I/O setup, explained in detail in Chapter 4, Preparing to Mix.

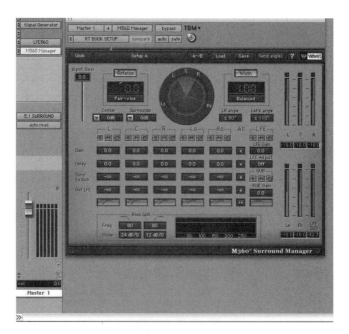

Fig. 2-5: Waves M360 plug-in

Calibrating with the Waves M360 Plug-In

1. Create a 5.1 Master Fader (File > New Track > Create 1 new > 5.1 > Master Fader), and assign the M360 to the last insert point. Then insert a multi-mono signal generator above the M360 set to –18dB level with Pink Noise as the Signal Source. On the M360, click on the Filter button at the bottom of each channel and LFE, directly under the "Get LFE" section. This inserts highpass and lowpass filters onto each channel.

2. Sit in the mix position and hold the SPL meter about chest high, angled up almost 45 degrees. Face it toward the Center speaker, and then on the M360, solo the Front Left channel.

3. Adjust the Front Left speaker, or M360, to your chosen reference level. I find 80dB easy to read on the SPL meter, so I generally set it there. Note that common mix levels are 85dB SPL for film, 79–80dB for TV, and anywhere from 75–84dB for music.

4. Proceed to solo each of the other two front channels (Center and Right), adjusting to 80dB. Make sure you face the Center speaker with the SPL meter while making all adjustments.

5. Once those are tweaked, it's time for the Left and Right Surrounds. While sitting in the same mix position as before, turn your body 90 degrees and face the SPL meter toward the left wall. Then solo the Left Surround channel and set it to 80dB. Follow the same steps for the Right Surround channel, again turning 90 degrees from center toward that speaker.

6. Now it's on to the Sub level. Solo the Sub and unmute the Center channel as well. You'll hear sound coming from the sub.

7. Adjust the Send To Sub so the level reads 6dB less than your chosen reference level. If your reference was 80dB, that would mean you want the meter to read 74dB. The reason you do this is simply that the sub has fewer overall frequency bands.

8. Follow this step for each of the remaining five speakers (Left, Right, Left Surround, and Right Surround).

9. Next, we will set the LFE level. Mute all speakers and the Sub.

10. On the M360, solo the LFE. Set the LFE Adjust to +10dB, and use the LFE Gain to raise the level until the SPL meter reads 4dB above the reference level (84dB if you're following the 80dB standard given above). Since there is 10dB of headroom on the LFE, you will now have a 10dB difference between the LFE and Sub level. Save this calibration as a preset. You're now ready to mix.

Bass Management

poor explanation! (handwritten margin note)

Most consumer home theater satellite speakers can't handle any audio information below 100Hz, so the crossovers in their receivers route that low-end signal to the subwoofer, along with any LFE information specific to that mix. If you have a matched set of five or more full-range speakers, you should make sure they can accurately reproduce all the frequencies of a bass-managed system. I've caught some serious low-end rumbles in several live mixes by listening with bass management engaged. If those frequencies weren't detected during mixing, the consumers at home may have gotten more low end than they bargained for.

Remember, bass management is an option that can be switched in and out (I use the Waves 360 Surround Bundle for this function), allowing professional mixers to monitor the way consumers might at home. *This is different from the speaker/sub crossover*, which should be set for your particular speaker and room setup. Re-read that again if it didn't make sense to you.

If you don't have the Waves 360 bundle in your Pro Tools rig to handle bass management functions, there are other options. Some monitoring systems have built-in bass management that can be set right on the speaker system itself. There are also relatively inexpensive external bass-management units available, such as the TMH Bass Manager or the Blue SKY BMC.

Consumer Surround: An Example

How Does Sound Get from Pro Tools to the Consumer?

This often-asked question has many answers. First you must examine your primary content—is it a live concert video, a special hi-resolution audio recording, or an ambient cue for a video game? Each project will probably have its own best delivery platform; i.e., a live concert would probably be best placed on DVD-Video. In contrast, a hi-resolution audio-only recording may work well as a DVD-Audio disc, with an included Dolby Digital and/or DTS layer for DVD-Video players. That same hi-res mix could also be made into a hybrid SA-CD, playing back the surround mix, stereo mix, and a 16-bit Red Book CD mix. Note again that for the SA-CD platform, a conversion from hi-bit PCM audio to DSD (Direct Stream Digital) will have to be done, usually at a mastering house. As for a video game ambience cue, it would most likely be for a gaming platform and would eventually be encoded/decoded into surround.

As a surround mixing engineer, it is your responsibility only to deliver the final multichannel mix (along with, usually, a stereo mix) to your client. They will then take your mixes and do what they need to do with them. Once that is out of the way, there is nothing you can do about it, and hopefully you delivered a great-sounding product (and have gotten paid for it). No matter what the format, though, a surround mix from Pro Tools will have to be encoded for each individual format and authored for public consumption.

Trying to Figure Out What the Consumers Will Hear: A Tough Task

As mentioned above, HTIB (Home Theater in a Box) is a huge market, selling millions of units a year. Even if consumers buy separate components and create their own systems, you will never know exactly how they will hear your mix. The variables are enormous, and may include the following:

- A setup with no Center channel.

- The surround speakers are too high or too low.

- A subwoofer is against a wall and is too loud.

- The subwoofer is set too low.

- One of the speakers is wired wrong and is out of phase.

- The receiver settings are incorrect.

- The Center speaker is mounted below a television.

- The speakers are too wide or too close together.

- The speakers are very small, with terrible frequency response and/or dynamic range.

Should I go on?

I simply think of these problems as issues the consumer is responsible for. Like stereo, where speakers may be wired wrong, misplaced, or blown, you can only mix surround for the optimum listening environment. It's your responsibility to do the best mix you can, and try to check it on as many systems as you can. Critics and fans have "panned" (pardon the pun) most surround mixing engineers at one time or another for not doing this or that right—but many also get praised for excellent work. Who knows what the consumer will hear? You can only take your best guess at it and mix for the masses to the best of your ability. Just make sure you start with a tuned room and go from there.

CHAPTER 3

Recording in Surround Sound

Getting Started

Recording in surround sound can be accomplished in several ways. As you would expect, the results you seek influence how you approach the session. Live and studio surround recording each has its own needs, as I will explain later in this chapter.

What Equipment Do You Need?

First and foremost, you have to get your sounds into Pro Tools. You can either use a microphone that records in surround, or simply record with traditional microphones keeping surround in mind. By this, I mean thinking and planning ahead as to where in your mix certain channels may be placed.

Recording Surround with Traditional Mics

By "traditional mics," I'm referring to microphones that record in either mono or stereo, which is most of them indeed! Again, I may sound like a broken record, but there is no right or wrong way. That's very important to remember, as it may guide you to try out new ideas without constraining to the traditions of the past.

Recording "traditionally" for surround could be as simple as placing a Shure SM57 on a guitar cabinet, then placing a large-diaphragm mic six feet back (or so) in the room. When mixing, you could possibly pan the SM57 to the Front Left channel. The ambient condenser mic could then be panned into the Rear Left channel, creating a true sense of space. You might even pan the room mic into the Rear Right channel, changing the image position. No rules—just try new ideas and have some fun.

Remember that any instrument can be recorded this way. Capturing acoustic guitars with a close and far mic is a wonderful technique. Try it also on vocals, percussion, horns, or piano. The only downside is the amount of recording channels and microphones you need. But don't forget—one of the great things about Pro Tools is that you can always add a few more channels! Try *that* with analog tape.

Another method for recording in surround is to use a four-channel (or more) microphone array. I've gotten some amazing results on drums, percussion, and string sections using this method, which reproduce beautifully in 5.1 when carefully recorded.

An Example: Surround Recording Using Traditional Mics on Drums

Apart from your conventional recording setup, such as kick, snare, toms, overheads, hi-hat, etc., you can place microphones around the kit to reproduce the sense of depth and space a room provides. I have had great success with Earthworks and DPA omni microphones, spaced about four feet in front of and in back of the kit, and about six feet apart (this is sometimes referred to as a "spaced-omni" setup). The height of each can be just above the cymbals, but make sure to set them high enough to capture the sense of height. In this application, the higher the quality of the microphone, the more realistic your sound will be on reproduction.

These "surround" mics are then panned into the four corners of your Pro Tools mix: Left, Right, Left Surround, and Right Surround, as if you were sitting in the

Fig: 3-1: An example of recording Surround with traditional mics

PRO TOOLS SURROUND SOUND MIXING

middle of the drum kit itself. The close mics used on the kit can then be mixed in any way you choose. Sometimes I've found the surround room mics to be so sonically exciting, you need very little of the close-mic kit recording. There are usually no phase issues involved because of the spacing of the microphones. Of course, you should always check your phase both during the recording and when you prepare to mix. Using this method, if you want to reproduce a smaller sonic footprint, just place the mics closer together. If you want a bigger image, simply place them farther apart and move them away from the source. You can also adjust your panning accordingly. As always, experimentation is key.

Listen to Your Room

When recording in surround, the quality of the actual room *sound* becomes extremely important. Don't forget that what you hear in the room can be reproduced quite accurately using four or more microphones. This aspect alone is one of my favorite benefits of surround sound. To capture a great drummer or pianist in a beautiful room and play back that sonic recording in 5.1 is an incredible experience. It adds so much to the power of a mix.

Often, in the pre-production stages of a surround project, I will discuss with the artist the merits of recording in a high-quality room. If the studio that houses that room is expensive, it may cost a little more to record, but the end results are always worth it. That's not to say that you have to go to a nice studio to record surround. You can literally use any room, but just think about the sonic results ahead of time. Wood rooms will sound like wood, tiled room like tile, and small rooms will sound small. Bathrooms, basements, garages, and stairwells can work nicely. As the saying goes, GIGO, or Garbage In, Garbage Out. I like to repeat my own saying: QIQO (Quality In, Quality Out). This truly applies to surround recording.

Fig. 3-2: Clubhouse Studios, Rhinebeck, New York

Monitoring While Recording Surround

This can get a little tricky. If you have a set of surround speakers in your recording environment, set them up! I usually carry my own set of speakers to a session to ensure that I can monitor in surround. This is obviously much easier in a studio or controlled environment, but many great engineers have set up makeshift surround monitoring systems in concert halls or mobile trucks for live gigs.

What I tend to do is set up for recording just like I mix. This means I have five speakers, plus a subwoofer, in the room. I route the Pro Tools outputs through my surround monitor controller or desk, and send them to the appropriate speakers. Be sure to run some tones and do a calibration (see Chapter 2). On rare occasions when time is tight, I have gotten away with simply playing back a mix I was familiar with to tune the room quickly by "ear." Don't tell anyone, though! This should only be done with experience. By properly tuning your recording setup, you can ensure a quality playback when you're mixing.

Certain elements of your recording need not be monitored in surround. But the things you do record in surround, such as drums, percussions, guitars, or horns, can benefit from surround monitoring while tracking. This can greatly aid in the microphone setup, as you can record and play back tests as you go along. It also gets the musicians excited when they walk into the control room after a take and hear their performance playing back in full surround. It's very inspirational.

As an example of surround monitoring, I will use the capturing of a drum kit. As mentioned in the section above, the kit is recorded as usual, but with the addition of four surround room mics.

Let's look at how each channel could be positioned:

Kick Inside: Panned center, divergence 50%

Kick Outside: Panned center, divergence 60%

Snare Top: Panned just right of center, divergence 50%

Snare Borrom: Panned just right of center, divergence 60%

Hi-Hats: Panned just left of center, divergence 30%

Tom High: Panned left front, divergence 90%

Tom Mid: Panned center, divergence 70%

Tom Low: Panned right front, divergence 90%

Overheads L/R: Panned left and right, slightly back in the soundfield, divergence 100%

Surround Front Left: Panned hard left front, divergence 100%

Surround Front Right: Panned hard right front, divergence 100%

Surround Rear Left: Panned hard left surround, divergence 100%

Surround Rear Right: Panned hard right surround, divergence 100%

This is a possible setup that will yield a nice wide, full sound. Note that the overheads are pulled slightly back off the front L/R pan position, and the Surround Front mics occupy the "hard" front L/R pan. The Surround Rear L/R microphones can be positioned anywhere in the surround field, depending on what result you are going for. I have found the "hard corner" pans with surround mics translate well on consumer playback systems. Also remember that this is just for monitoring during recording; the mix positions can always be changed at a later date.

Microphones That Record in Surround

There are several microphones available that record in surround. This normally means they can output four or more channels from the same setup. Microphones such as this can yield some amazing results by themselves, or in conjunction with other mics. One of the major benefits of using a surround microphone, or microphone array, is the incredible detail and imaging that can be achieved from one simple, compact setup.

Each mic type will have its own set of requirements. Let's take a look at a few examples of surround microphones.

The SoundField System

www.soundfieldusa.com
www.transaudio.com

Fig. 3-3: SoundField inside capsule

Fig. 3-4: SoundField SP451 Surround Processor

The SoundField system offers the ability to record in surround with one microphone. The technology behind this product is based on the principle that all acoustic events can be represented by four basic elements, as follows:

- "X" represents front/back information (depth)

- "Y" is left/right information (width)

- "Z" is up/down information (height)

- "W" is the central point from which all the other elements are referred.

This joint combination of X, Y, Z, and W is referred to collectively as "B-Format." SoundField mics are the only microphones that generate B-Format. The sound from a B-Format microphone is captured at one center point. Therefore, all output variations, from mono thru 5.1 and 6.1, are derived from the same source.

B-Format output from a SoundField microphone is fed into the SP451 hardware controller, which is able to remotely generate a wide variety of sonic nuances, all from the single microphone setup. By the time you read this book, SoundField will have a Surround Zone plug-in for Pro Tools available.

Here's a list of some of the basic benefits users get from using the SoundField system:

- The SoundField system is literally several microphones in one. A single Sound-Field mic is:

  - A studio-grade mono condenser microphone that can be cardioid, omni, hypercardioid, figure-8, or anything in-between.

  - A stereo condenser microphone with stereo cardioid, stereo omni, stereo hypercardioid, and stereo figure-8.

  - A surround microphone which, in conjunction with the SP451 Surround Sound Processor or Surround Zone software plug-in, can generate 5.1, 6.1, and 7.1 formats.

- Users have remote control over the continuous patterns. Patterns and their associated variations are controlled by a single stereo rotary pot, beginning with omni and narrowing to hypercardioid, ending in figure-8. SoundField's B-Format processing supplies identical L/R patterns regardless of the X/Y angle, which they refer to as "width." This width can vary from mono to extra-wide stereo.

- Because this setup generates all its sound from a single point source, there are no phase summing errors when folding down to stereo, or even mono.

- The Surround Zone plug-in lets you change all the microphone parameters even after you've recorded, by using Patter, Tilt, Zone, and End Fire controls. In essence, you can alter your sound to make it more or less ambient, tighter, or wider.

I've recorded in surround with the SoundField system, and the results are amazing. I once hung an MKV system out the window in the middle of New York City and recorded four channels of output to Pro Tools. Using the SP451 Surround Processor, I was able to generate an incredibly realistic 5.1 experience; if you closed your eyes and just listened, you would swear you were standing in the street.

The SPL Atmos 5.1 Surround Miking System, Model 9843

www.soundperformancelab.com

Another type of surround microphone system is the Atmos 5.1 controller with a Brauner ASM5 Adjustable Surround Microphone. This setup is based upon five matched microphone heads from the Brauner VM 1 microphone.

The ASM5 positions the Left/Center/Right microphone heads in a rectangle triangle, each microphone being 17.5cm away from the center. Polar pattern characteristics can be remotely changed from the Atmos 5.1 controller, from omni thru figure-8. The microphone head positions are variable ±90 degrees.

The Atmos 5.1 controller has five precision preamps that can be gain-adjusted with one control, essential while recording live. It also features a Front/Surround and L/C/R pan control with divergence to change the imaging when needed, as well as stereo spreading. The .1 channel can be summed from the Front, Surround, and Center channels—there is a –24dB Butterworth lowpass filter at 130Hz. If the filter is not activated, a mono composite can be sent to a separate LFE/Sub processor. This ultimately gives you more control over the low end of the recording.

Note that any microphone setup can be used with the Atmos 5.1 controller.

The Holophone H2 Pro

www.holophone.com

This easy-setup "point-and-shoot" microphone array captures up to 7.1 channels (Left, Center, Right, Left Surround, Right Surround, Center Rear, and Top, for IMAX applications). Apart from music applications, it is suitable for television (DTV, HDTV, and standard TV), field ENG, gaming, and film work. The output is real-time discrete and it features eight individual microphone elements powered by

DPA mics. The elliptical shape emulates a human head, so the sound waves "bend" to provide a completely natural sound experience.

An Overvew: Recording Surround Live

Classical music lends itself particularly well to live surround captures. Taking advantage of the fine acoustic spaces and musicianship, engineers use a variety of methods, including any combination of surround microphones over the conductor, multiple audience microphones, standard Decca Trees, stage microphones, and mics hanging from the ceiling. The mics are typically very high quality, with high-quality preamps. They can be any mixture of cardioid or omni, a choice the producers and engineers make ahead of time. Surround microphones, if used, are usually combined with the traditional mics.

Many if not all of today's concert DVDs include some form of surround track. Not only does it add a sonic value, but also it adds production value to the overall package. A full 5.1 Dolby AC-3 stream is the most common form of surround delivered, but DTS tracks are often included to give the consumer a choice.

I've recorded several live concerts that have been released in surround. One event in particular, *Romero's Live at Trinity Church, New York*, makes a good case study for this book. The event took place in New York's historic Trinity Church, in front of a live audience assembled just for the recording. Amazingly enough, the church has a full-blown Pro Tools studio upstairs, tie-lined to the pulpit. We set the band up right there on the pulpit, and close-miked all the instruments with a variety of excellent microphones and preamps. For the surround channels, I used a stereo pair of Earthworks QTC-1 omni microphones, set up about six feet off the stage and 20 feet apart. These two microphones captured the sonic reflections of an incredible acoustic space, and truly helped define the sound of the record.

For the multichannel SA-CD release on 333 Entertainment, we mixed the band as if they were set up on the pulpit, just as they were positioned during the actual concert. I placed the two Earthworks audience mics into the surround channels, panned hard Left Surround and hard Right Surround. This created a true sense of space and depth, as if the listener was sitting five rows back in the church.

Listen to Romero's "El Reynado" example on the DVD to hear a live surround recording.

Using the Surround Channels in Stereo

Another benefit I found in recording additional surround-channel information is their use in stereo. In both live and studio recordings, I've transformed the surround elements into realistic reverb.

When doing a stereo mix, one approach is to blend the extra channels in with the original source. For example, in some live recordings, I've taken the two or more distant microphones and placed them low (in volume) in the stereo mix. This creates a beautiful sense of space, utilizing real acoustic ambience, early reflections, and unique tonality to add dimension to the mix. Once again, there are no phase issues due to the distance from the original source (when using split omni/cardioid microphones). The amount of "surround" sound you add to your mix then becomes a matter of taste.

With studio recordings being mixed in stereo, I often use the Rear Surround microphones to add the same type of depth, especially with drums and/or percussion. It's like having another reverb in your mix, only each one is sonically unique.

Preparing to Mix in Surround

4

The Surround Mixer Plug-In

Before you begin, make sure the Surround Mixer plug-in is installed in your Plug-Ins folder. If not, either find it on your Pro Tools Installer CD-ROM, or go online and download the latest version for your setup.

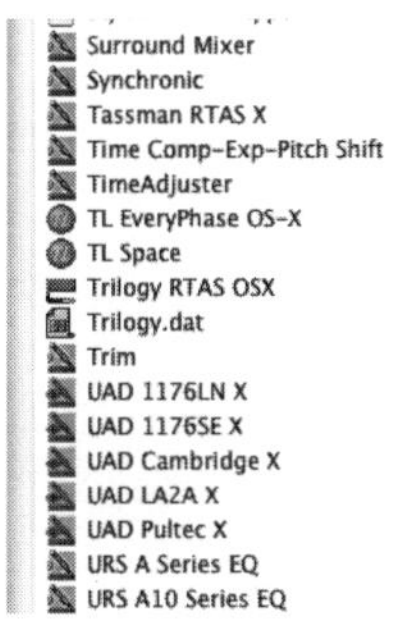

Surround Mixer
Synchronic
Tassman RTAS X
Time Comp-Exp-Pitch Shift
TimeAdjuster
TL EveryPhase OS-X
TL Space
Trilogy RTAS OSX
Trilogy.dat
Trim
UAD 1176LN X
UAD 1176SE X
UAD Cambridge X
UAD LA2A X
UAD Pultec X
URS A Series EQ
URS A10 Series EQ

Fig. 4-1: Surround Mixer plug-in

Setting up Pro Tools to do a surround mix can be a bit confusing the first few times. But, like anything else, you get used to the process and it becomes second nature. The guide that comes with your Pro Tools software is a good place to start. There are several chapters offering excellent explanations of how to get your Pro Tools system ready to produce surround sound. One of the most important concepts to understand is the I/O Setup window (found under the "Setups" menu). It is also important to know that, like most other functions in Pro Tools, there are usually several ways to achieve the same objective.

Think of the I/O Setup simply as a path to get your audio to the speakers, one channel at a time. With stereo, you would route the left channel to the left speaker, and the right channel to the right speaker. When mixing in surround, however, it just so happens that you now need to route more than two channels. Below, I'll explain a few of the simplest ways that I've found for setting Pro Tools up for multichannel mixing.

The I/O Setup Window

The I/O Setup and the Channel Grid are like having a huge patchbay, but without the cables (or even the patchbays!). First you must decide on what surround format you will mix to. Typically, a 5.1 session would need a 5.1 I/O setting.

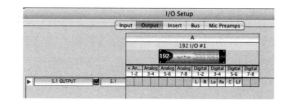

Fig. 4-2: The I/O setup

Whether you are remixing a stereo session or creating a new surround mix, you must configure Pro Tools for surround. You can either create a new I/O Setup, or import one.

To import a multichannel I/O Setup, do the following:

1. Go to Setups > I/O Setup.

4. Click on Import Settings.

5. Select an I/O settings file to import.

Note that if the current session has existing paths that overlap the imported settings, Pro Tools will ask whether you want to delete them, or whether you want to retain them and add them to your session. Click No to add these paths and Yes to replace them.

I keep a selection of 5.1 I/O Setups ready to be imported whenever I start a new session. This lets me quickly get to work without going through the hassle of a new setup each time. I simply name it 5.1 Surround, and it already has all the relevant Outputs, Inputs, Busses, and Inserts I may need. To Export an I/O setup you have created, do the following:

1. Go to Setups > I/O Setup.

2. Click on Export Settings.

3. Name and Save the I/O Setting.

Multichannel paths and sub-paths are mapped to inputs, outputs, and busses in the Channel Grid. The I/O Setup dialog also lets you route the physical inputs and outputs on your audio interface (192 or 888 for surround) to available inputs and outputs in Pro Tools.

Here's a look at the Output tab of the I/O Setup dialog:

Meter: This selects the path shown in the meters of a control surface. I always leave it at the default setting "1-8," therefore showing the channel output meters of channels 1 through 8.

Audition: This selects the monitor path for previewing audio in the Regions List, Import Audio dialog, and DigiBase. Note that you can only use outputs on your primary audio interface for this. For example, when you preview a sample of audio, this will define what outputs that sample is heard through.

Default Output: This selects the default output path for new tracks for each format. If you've named your I/O Output "My 5.1 Surround," the Default Output will show up on your channel strip as "My 5.1 Surround."

Default Path Order: Selects the default path order for 5.1 paths. The options are L C R LS RS LFE (Film), L R C LFE Ls Rs (SMPTE/ITU), or L R Ls Rs C LFE (DTS/ProControl Monitoring). On my setup at home, I set this to L R Ls Rs C LFE for use with ProControl.

Here is a chart of the surround mix I/O Settings files provided for three specific track layout standards:

5.1 Setting	Track Layout
Film (Pro Tools Standard)	L C R Ls Rs LFE
SMPTE/ITU (Control 24 Monitoring)	L R C LFE Ls Rs
DTS (ProControl Monitoring)	L R Ls Rs C LFE

Creating a New 5.1 I/O Setup with Subpaths

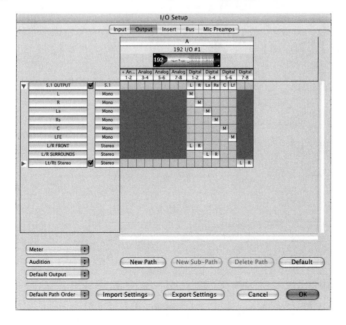

Fig. 4-3: I/O Setup with subpaths and L/R mix on 7.8.

1. Go to Setups > I/O Setup.

2. Click on the Outputs Tab > select New Path.

3. Choose 5.1 from the dropdown menu.

4. Click on box 1 in the I/O Grid. Pro Tools will create six outputs, labeled L, C, R, Ls, Rs, and LFE.

5. Double-click the Name Grid and call it 5.1 Surround.

6. If this is the output path you desire, do nothing. If not, simply click and drag the channels to your chosen position (for example, changing the output order to L, R, Ls, Rs, C, LFE).

7. Click on the Default Path Order to confirm your physical hardware output order.

8. For the subpaths, click New Sub-Path eight times.

9. Create six mono subpaths, one for each of these channels: L, C, R, Ls, Rs, LFE. Then create two stereo subpaths, for the following: L, R and Ls, Rs.

10. Click > New Path and create one stereo path on Grid outputs 7 and 8. Name it Stereo Mix.

11. Name and Export this setup by clicking Export Settings. Now you'll have it for later use.

This is the I/O setup that I use the most. It gives you flexibility with routing to the 5.1 Surround output, a stereo Left/Right, a Surround L/R, or a separate Stereo Mix. If you follow the Film/Pro Tools Standard output configuration, your mix out of Pro Tools will follow this path.

Pro Tools Physical Outputs

- CH 1: Left Front

- CH 2: Center

- CH 3: Right Front

- CH 4: Left Surround

- CH 5: Right Surround

- CH: 6 LFE

- CH 7: Left output of Stereo Mix

- CH 8: Right output of Stereo Mix

After I create the I/O Output setup, I typically create and name my Bus configurations for the session. That would usually include several 5.1 reverbs, several Quad reverbs for my Impulse Responses, some stereo and mono delays, and a few traditional stereo reverbs. Other elements are added as needed.

Some engineers at this point may also create I/O Setup Output stems for additional mixes. These stems are usually printed at unity gain, and re-combined in post-production to offer additional flexibility. For example, a Dolby Pro Logic mix might utilize a three-channel LCR sub-path and a mono left/right surround sub-path. Or for multichannel film or commercial work, there might be sub-path stems for music, Foley, dialog, and/or effects.

Multichannel Audio Tracks

Multichannel tracks are not required to mix in surround—you can easily create a surround mix from mono and stereo tracks. However, there are times when multichannel tracks are quite useful. When creating a standard 5.1 track, the layout and metering conforms to the film standard: L C R Ls Rs LFE.

Fig. 4-4: 5.1 Audio Tracks

In the I/O Setup window, you can route these signals out of your interface in accordance with any track layout simply by clicking and dragging them to a relevant location in the I/O Grid.

A 5.1 audio track is actually six channels, all under the control of one fader, mute, and solo switch. What's more, a multichannel track can be edited and processed like any other track. Note that complete six-channel mixes can be imported into a 5.1 track. When finishing a full surround project, I often import all the material into one 5.1 track. That helps me listen to the songs in quick succession, experiment with processing, or get an idea of ordering before going to mastering. Also, when tracks come back from mastering, I can import them into that 5.1 track and play them out of my Pro Tools system.

Audio files and regions can be dragged into a multichannel audio track from the Regions List. The number of channels of audio simply has to match the destination track format. For example, a quad setup of four audio channels must be dragged to a quad audio track, two-channel to a stereo track, etc.

It's important to name your tracks, since the files you drag in appear in that order, from top to bottom. If you don't name them, and the output is arranged differently than the tracks, you will hear them incorrectly. For individual control over multichannel tracks, you must convert them to mono by doing the following:

1. Choose the multichannel track you wish to convert.

2. Select File > Split Selected Tracks to Mono.

Multichannel Track Outputs

Assigning a track output will determine the format of that specific channel's output. When you click and hold the output of a channel, you will see the tab pop up offering "no output," "interface," or "bus," with the corresponding arrow to a dropdown menu selection. For a 5.1 surround setup with an I/O Output labeled "5.1 Output," you would select interface > 5.1 Output.

If your channel is mono, Pro Tools will automatically assign the channel a mono surround panner. A stereo channel would get a stereo panner, and a 5.1 channel would get no panner, but would be assigned six meters. The reason there is no panner on a 5.1 channel is because you can't pan a 5.1 track—the audio on a 5.1 track is assigned to the corresponding L, R, C, Ls, Rs, and LFE outputs in the Pro Tools session. Most if not all tracks in a surround mix are mono or stereo, which can be panned accordingly.

You can always tell what kind of track you have by looking at the number of meters in the fader strip. A 5.1 track will have six discrete meters, just as a stereo track will have two.

Since multiple paths can be assigned for a channel, the main output for the track will match the format of the path with the largest number of channels. To add an additional output assignment to a track:

• Control-click the Selector and assign another path (Mac)

• Ctrl-click the Selector and assign another path (Windows)

Tracks can be routed to bus paths or multichannel outputs via the track Output Selector. Pro Tools will then assign it a multichannel panner and associated meter in both the Mix and Edit windows.

Multichannel Master Fader

Only one Master Fader can be active in any single Main path at once, although it can be assigned to both Main and Subpath outputs. This Master fader is where you would insert your plug-in processing to affect the entire mix. For example, the Waves 360 Manager and LFE Filter are normally assigned to a Master Fader. Automated fade-ins or fade-outs can be done using the Master Fader, which will obviously affect the entire mix assigned to that output.

Multichannel Plug-Ins

You'll find a comprehensive look at many multichannel plug-ins in Chapter 9, Software Plug-Ins for Surround Sound. Note that plug-ins can be multichannel, mono, or multi-mono.

Multichannel plug-ins are designed for use on multichannel tracks. When correlated processing is needed, a multichannel plug-in should be chosen. Multi-mono plug-ins can be used on stereo or larger-than-stereo tracks. Not all correlated multichannel plug-ins allow for individual channel adjustments, so this is where you might want to use a multi-mono plug-in instead. Also, not all plug-ins (in fact, not many) support multichannel processing.

The controls are linked when first inserting a multi-mono plug-in on a multichannel track. To unlink them, simply deselect the master button (it looks like two crossed ovals). This button remains lit when linked and unlit when unlinked. You can utilize the channel selector in a multi-mono plug-in to edit its parameters. Also, by Option-clicking (on a Mac) or Alt-clicking (on Windows computers) the Channel Selector, you can open a plug-in window for all channels.

Multichannel Sends

You can assign one or more multichannel sends to any track format, from mono upwards. This will then show a multichannel panner in the Sends View, which can be used to bus tracks to plug-ins or create additional independent mixes.

Multichannel Aux Inputs/Outputs

A multichannel Auxiliary Input is used to return a multichannel bus. In order to use a multichannel reverb, for example, you should create a stereo aux input. When instantiating a reverb such as the Waves R360 5.1, Pro Tools automatically creates a six-channel aux output so that the reverb is heard in all six speakers of a 5.1 mix, including the LFE.

Panners

Digidesign Surround Panner

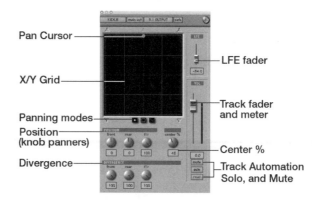

Fig. 4-5: Digidesign mono surround panner

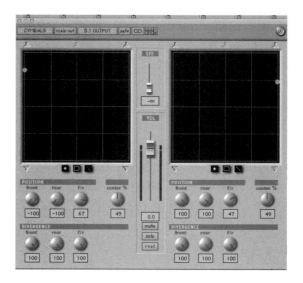

Fig. 4-6: Digidesign stereo surround panner

Currently, there are four panning methods available when mixing surround sound in Pro Tools. You can use the full-size Digi panner in the Output Window, the reduced-height panner in the Mix Window, the reduced-height panner in the Edit Window's I/O view, or by using automation editing. Let's take a look at the surround panner that Digidesign provides for mixing.

To open a panner in the Output window, click on the output icon in the Mix or Edit window (it sits right above the level meter). When assigned to tracks that have four or more channels, the panner window provides an X/Y Grid (see panner above). The speaker icons provided are also associated with the multichannel format selected and will be displayed accordingly.

Center Percentage

Center Percentage is a very important feature in this panner. It controls whether the Center channel is discrete or phantom. As you reduce the value below its preset of 100%, the Center speaker icon becomes less visible. At 0%, it's not there, meaning that the image is now a phantom Center. Typically, I work with values around 50% so that the associated speakers around the Center speaker will help carry the audio image. Relying on the Center channel alone to carry information is not recommended in surround mixing (unless you want to take a chance or go for a specific effect). Remember, not all consumers will have it set up correctly, if they have it at all.

poor explanation

The X/Y Grid

Pan information can be input into the grid using X/Y, 3-Knob, or numeric value mode. Multichannel panners default to X/Y Mode, visible on the Panning Modes selector just below the X/Y Grid. The small green dot (the pan cursor) indicates current pan position in this mode. It will turn red when in Automation Write, Touch, or Latch Mode, and yellow when in Trim or Auto Off Mode.

Panning Modes

X/Y Mode can be activated by selecting the X/Y Mode button (farthest to the left). This is joystick-style panning, allowing you to move the cursor anywhere within the grid. Click anywhere in the grid to move the pan position, or click on a speaker to jump the cursor to it.

3-Knob Panning is activated by selecting the right-most icon with the diagonal slash. This allows for point-to-point panning between discrete pairs of speakers or in straight lines using the rotary knobs. For example, you can pan from the Front Right speaker to the Left Surround speaker in a straight line—with audio coming only from those speakers. 3-Knob panning works with a panning trajectory, whereas X/Y panning works in the full field of 360 degrees.

To pan in 3-Knob mode:

1. Enable 3-Knob panning in the Panning Modes section.

2. Adjust Front and Rear Position Knobs to create your trajectory path.

3. Rotate the Front/Rear Position knob, and the cursor will pan only on the white trajectory line.

4. Drag either endpoint of the trajectory line to change the angle, or simply adjust the Front or Rear Position controls.

Position Controls

These let you set the position of the panner. The selections are: Front, Rear, and F/R (front/rear).

- Front controls and displays the X-axis, or Left/Right position.

- Rear controls and displays the rear X-axis of the panner, or Rear Left/Right position. Note that in X/Y panning mode, Rear is linked to the Front position and cannot be independently controlled.

- F/R (Front/Rear) controls and displays the Y-axis position of the panner.

LFE Fader

This fader controls how much LFE information from the selected track is sent to the subwoofer. It's available only when a track is assigned to a path that supports it (such as 5.1). Note that this fader is fully automatable.

Divergence

Divergence provides control over the "width" of a panned signal. With Divergence set to 100% on a panner (known as full divergence), the signal will be heard only in the speaker it is assigned to.

When you lower the divergence below 100%, the sound of that signal will spread out across the speakers adjacent to it. On the Digidesign Panner, there are Front (controlling the Front speakers on the X-axis), Rear (Rear speakers X-axis only) and F/R Divergence (controlling the Front Rear Y-axis) options.

On the panners, there are three divergence controls: Front, Rear, and F/R (Front/Rear), along with their associated knob controls and values. The current divergence values are displayed in the grid using a purple outline. The panner sets all values at 100% (fully divergent) by default.

To adjust panner divergence, click the Divergence icon (the small rectangle in the middle) of the Panning Modes section. By lowering divergence values, you can hear your signal get wider (by bleeding it into adjacent speakers). This is useful to cover a wide area with a sound source. Move the controls around to experiment.

If you hold down the Command key (Mac) or Ctrl key (Windows), you can have fine adjustment of all panner controls. Also, by Option-clicking (Mac) or Alt-clicking (Windows) in the Panner Grid, you can reset all controls to default. All pan controls can be fully automated, including divergence, LFE, and pan position.

Stereo Panning

Stereo pans can be linked or unlinked by clicking on the two-ovals icon just to the right of the Safe button. By selecting any one of the three arrows (two Left/Right, one Front/Back), the pans can be linked to work in various configurations, including opposite each other, together, Front/Back, and opposite Front/Back. Experiment to see which mode works best for your application.

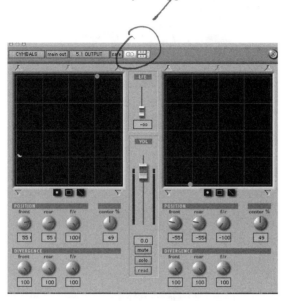

Fig. 4-7: Digidesign Stereo Panner in Linked Mode

Assigning a Digidesign Surround Panner

1. Make sure your I/O Setup has a surround output assigned, with a name such as "5.1 OUTPUT."

2. On the output of the track you want to assign it to, click and hold until you find "5.1 OUTPUT."

3. A Digidesign surround panner will appear just below the Automation box— a mono track will automatically have a mono panner, stereo will have a stereo panner, etc.

Waves Surround Panner & Imager

The Waves S360 is a surround panning and imaging tool, for either 5.0 or 5.1 channels. The S360 Panner lets you set Width and Rotation for a mono, stereo, 5.0, or 5.1 surround source. The S360 Imager is actually an enhanced panner which

Fig. 4-8: Waves Surround Panner

adds Room Model early reflections to create distance panning, as well as a Shuffling function for additional low-frequency width.

These tools can be used to complement Digidesign's X/Y panners in a surround mix, since their functionality is slightly different. Like having various EQs or reverbs, these are simply optional ways to pan your sources. The S360 Panner is intended to be placed on a track's last insert; this allows for processing to happen pre-panner.

The S360 Imager has the same feature set as the Panner, but it adds Distance Panning and Shuffling parameters (at the cost of slightly more DSP overhead). Therefore, the Imager should be used if you have a source that you want to create a sense of distance with. It's especially effective when creating room simulations. You can specify the distance desired in the ER section, which has the following choices:

- **ER Absorb:** Controls a highpass shelf filter on the Early Reflection path, allowing you to set how bright or dull you'd like the sound to be.

- **Frequency:** The ER Absorb's cutoff frequency; cutting off high frequencies will provide a "darker" sound.

- **Distance/Room size link:** Sets the relationship between Distance and Room size. Can be linked or unlinked. When linked, Distance is controlled by the Room size.

- **Front/Rear:** Lets you create a sensation of being in a room, where the ERs will be dominant in either the front or rear stage.

There is a large Rotation Graph in the middle of the panner, with markers to control Rotation, Width, and Distance. The Rotation section actually has three controls: Rotation On/Off, Angle, and Pan Pot. You can choose Pair-wise or Triple-wise (Pair-wise is the default). At the bottom of each Panner or Imager is also a Solo section where you can click and listen to each channel's output on its own, indicated by the associated speaker icon turning on or off.

The Width section also has three controls: Width On/Off, Width Ratio, and Width Pan Pot. The Pan Pot is interesting in that it lets you select Mono Divergence, Balanced, Front-Stage, Focus, or Front/Rear stage. Center % allows the Center speaker to be used discretely, or you can take a phantom center and feed it equally into the Left and Right speakers at –3dB. Below that sits the Send to LFE control, which directs the track's audio to the LFE channel at the selected amount of gain (similar the the LFE slider on the Digi panner).

When using the Imager, there will also be an Early Reflections graph (showing timing and levels) above the Rotation Graph. Inside the Rotation Graph is a directional energy meter that displays the same information as the output peak meters, which sit to the right of the circle. Also on the Imager is a section to control Shuffle and Frequency. Shuffling widens the bass frequencies, and this control will change the amount that will occur below the value indicated in the Frequency Control. Shuffler can be turned on or off for easy before-and-after comparison.

Fig. 4-9: Waves Imager

Because it has only Early Reflections present, the Imager is meant to combine with the R360 Surround Reverb, which will provide the tail to that sound. Waves provides a number of S360 Imager and R360 Reverb presets that complement one another and are designed to be used in tandem. For example, each plug-in has something called "Small Bright Room" under the "Virtual Spaces" menu. When you select it, the Imager will handle the room simulation and the Reverb will handle the tails. The combination is quite powerful.

As you can tell, the Waves 360 Panner provides many options for surround mixing. I usually find myself using a combination of Digidesign panners, 360 Panners, and 360 Imagers for most mixes. Also, check out the enclosed DVD for an example of how the Imager sounds on an audio track.

Assigning a Waves Panner/Imager

The Waves Panner or Imager is instantiated as a plug-in, unlike the Digidesign panner, which is placed on an output. The choices (for stereo or surround) are S360 Panner (stereo/5.0), S360 Imager (stereo/5.0), S360 Panner (stereo/5.1), or S360 Imager (stereo/5.1). A mono panner would read Mono. To assign a Waves Panner or Imager:

1. Click on the last insert and instantiate a Waves Panner or Imager.

2. The Panner or Imager will appear onscreen and the channel configuration and metering will change accordingly. For a stereo source, you would see it play back in stereo on the channel's meters. As you pan the source, the meters will reflect the changes in the energy field.

3. If you had a Digidesign panner on the channel previously, it will automatically be removed and replaced with the Waves Panner/Imager. Be careful, though, because it may remove any sends you have on the channel (however, plug-ins will remain instantiated). For that reason, I always try to assign panners before I process.

4. If you assigned an S360 Panner and decided to use an Imager instead, simply instantiate the Imager. The Panner's parameters and positions will show up on the Imager, only you will now have the additional controls.

Panning in Surround

Once your I/O is set up correctly, you can assign a surround panner to a channel. You can then use it to place the sounds in the multichannel field. Note that not every channel in a mix needs to be given a multichannel output panner. Should you choose not to assign an element to a surround panner, you can simply route it to an output sub-path (often called a "hard assign"). Here are a few examples and potential approaches to each:

• Let's say you have a mono vocal track. You could assign a Digidesign Surround Panner to it, and place it only in the Center channel, using full divergence (read explanation above). With this approach, you'll hear that vocal only in that one channel. If you panned it to the Left speaker, you would only hear it there, and if you panned it to the Right Surround speaker, you'd only hear it

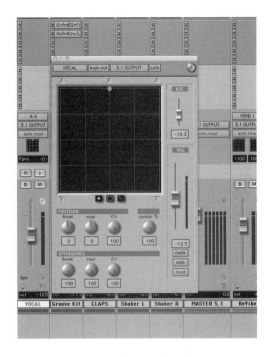

Fig. 4.10: Mono Surround Panner Center % 100 percent

in that speaker. If you choose to, you can automate it to make circles around your head. See Figure 4.10 above and listen to Audio Example 1 on the DVD to hear a vocal, with 100% Center only.

DVD Example 1: Mono Vocal, Center Channel Only

- Another option is to take that same vocal, set the divergence at 50%, and "spread out the image" across the Left, Center, and Right channels. This approach is quite useful, as I've found it creates a nice, full vocal spread for a consumer to hear on a home playback system. Remember, not everyone will have the Center channel set up correctly, if they have one installed at all! Sometimes I will pull the channel's Pan Cursor back toward the middle of the soundfield, creating further depth. However, this may also "wash out" the image, so be careful—you might have to boost the volume to compensate. Audio Example 2 on the DVD is a vocal based in the center channel, diverged at 50%, and slightly pulled back into the soundfield.

- Also note that if you did not use a surround panner and assigned this vocal channel to the L/R mix, you would hear it only in the Left and Right speakers. The vocal would therefore be a "phantom center" image. If you had a Center channel subpath Send on your I/O setup, you could output it that way as well (and it would only be in the Center channel). With both of these, you would also lose any surround controls such as divergence, center percentage, or position.

Create a New Session

Once you have configured your I/O Setup, it's time to get to work. A typical surround session will usually have the exact same basic elements of a stereo session. They would be stereo and mono tracks, a Master Fader, Auxiliary inputs for reverbs, and effects and busses. The difference becomes apparent when you create a Surround Master Fader or assign any Surround Panners and/or Surround Aux inputs.

Use an Existing Session

Many Pro Tools surround mixing sessions begin by simply opening up the stereo mix. One of the benefits to this method is that all the automation is already there, much of which can be applied to the surround mix. Therefore, much of the overall work may already be done.

As an example, if you had a vocal phantom centered (at equal level in the Left and Right speakers) in your stereo mix and then put a surround panner on it, your volume automation and any send information would still be there. Even any Left/Right stereo pan movements you might have made would reproduce on the surround panner. You could then choose to change the Center percentage or divergence, or move it to the Rear speakers if you want.

One of the first steps I take in converting an existing stereo mix to surround is to import a previously saved 5.1 I/O setup into a stereo session. This will have all my input and output assigns, plus all my bus information. Next, I would assign surround panners to any elements I knew needed them, and create several aux sends with surround plug-ins on them. The other channels that do not need panners can remain static. That means that I could either "hard assign" them to a specific output (say L/R mix), or create a sub-path in the I/O setup and route it that way.

Next, I might create a bank of surround reverbs to use. For me, it would typically involve creating a Waves 360 5.1 Reverb channel, an Altiverb Quad channel, and a 5.1 Digidesign ReVibe channel, among others. Going back to that vocal, you could then send some of it to one of those surround reverbs, creating that immersive feeling that only multichannel mixing can provide. However, you could also utilize stereo and mono delays and reverbs to create some nice-sounding placements.

At this point, if I had ambient room microphones recorded along with the drums, I would then either assign surround panners to them or route them to a stereo L/R Surround sub-path from my I/O setup. I would then mix the rest of the drum kit accordingly, usually focusing it primarily across the front three speakers. Then the rest of the elements would be positioned where they needed to be.

Every mix is different, and every mixer's approach is different. Sometimes I even assign a surround panner to every single channel and work "backwards," taking careful note of the default Center percentage of each. One of my criteria for surround mixing is to ask myself if the mix is more exciting than the stereo one (if there is one at all!)—if so, I know I'm on the right path. Another question I ask myself is, have I provided the listener with an experience that could not be reproduced in stereo? Once I have achieved that, it's all personal preference.

Simple Step-By-Step Creation of a Surround Mix from Stereo

1. Open up a stereo session as normal. For this example, I will open up a 60-second TV spot I did some time ago.

2. Go to Setups > I/O Setup > Output tab.

3. Create a New Path. Select 5.1 from the dropdown menu, and click in the Grid Box to create a six-channel output. Uncheck Stereo outputs 1–2, 3–4, 5–6, and 7–8. Click OK in I/O Setup box.

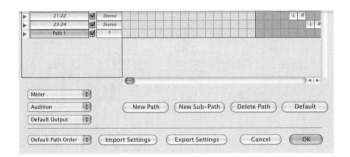

Fig. 4-11: "Check your default path order"

4. Make sure the Default Path Order reads L,C,R, Ls, Rs, LFE (for this example). Note that the 5.1 Output in the Grid Box follows the same order.

5. As you can see below, all the Channel Outputs are now greyed out, since we de-selected Output 1–2 and created the 5.1 Output.

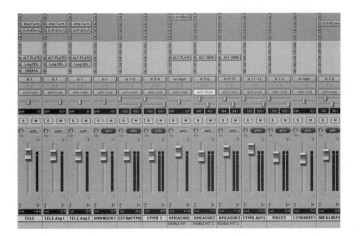

Fig. 4-12: Greyed-out channel outputs

6. In the Mix Window, select channel output, then select Interface > 5.1 Output. Notice that a Digidesign Surround Panner appears on Channel 1 TELE.

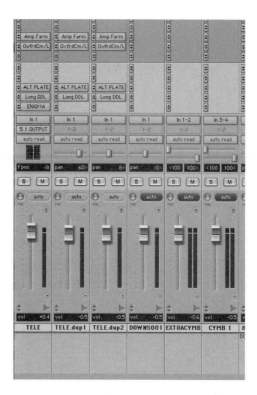

Fig. 4-13: Channel 1 output with Digi Panner

7. Select File > New Track > Create 1 new 5.1 Master Fader > Create

Fig. 4-14: New Master Fader

8. Notice the new 5.1 Master Fader, which will control all channels sent out the 5.1 Output.

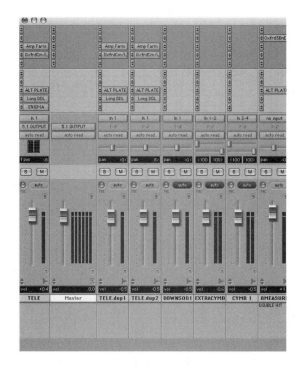

Fig. 4-15: New Master Fader in Mix window

9. Go back to Setups > I/O Setup > Output tab. Select 5.1 Output until it lights up blue, then click New Sub-Path two times.

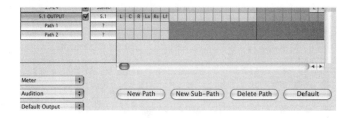

Fig. 4-16: Two new sub-paths

10. Create two Stereo sub-paths, and click on either the L or R Grid to create an L/R sub-path, then click on either Ls or Rs to create a new Ls/Rs sub-path. Name each one in the sub-path box.

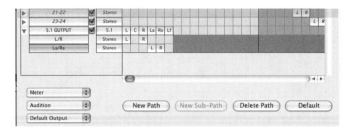

Fig. 4-17: New sub-path names

11. This provides additional outputs besides the 5.1 Output. You can now "hard patch" channels to the L/R or Ls/Rs output, should you choose not to put a surround panner on it. You can then assign the next few channels to the L/R mix; they will be heard on the Left and Right speakers with a phantom center image. The two stereo channels for cymbals will then get assigned to the 5.1 Output, calling up stereo Digidesign Surround Panners.

Fig. 4-18: Assigning L/R outputs and Digi Panners

From there, I would typically assign the rest of the tracks to their respective panners and positions in the mix. Then I would assign a Waves 360 LFE and Waves M360 Manager to the last two inserts of the 5.1 Master Fader to handle bass management. The mix would then get some surround reverbs, stereo and mono reverbs and delays, and additional processing as usual. Note that when creating a surround reverb, you first have to create a stereo aux input; then, by assigning the multichannel TDM plug-in, it automatically creates a six-channel aux input for the effect.

Fig. 4-19: Final mix configuration

What's the Difference Between Sub & LFE?

It's actually quite simple. LFE, or ".1", is a channel of audio you can mix to. That's why you'll often hear it called the Low Frequency Effects *channel.* The subwoofer is something physical, an actual speaker on the floor that reproduces the LFE channel. The subwoofer also handles any low-end signal your main speakers cannot; this signal is routed away from them via bass management (see below).

When your Pro Tools surround mix is played back on a consumer system, the subwoofer will carry the following information:

• Any LFE information you created in your mix. The only way to do this is with the LFE slider (on either the Digidesign or Waves Surround Panner).

• Any other low-frequency signal that your bass management filter sends to the sub. Remember, many speakers cannot handle information below even 120Hz; all those frequencies and below, from all the channels you've mixed, will be cut off and routed to the sub. Some systems also offer bass re-direction, in case you have full-range speakers and choose to use them. For example, if you had two full-range speakers for the Left and Right Fronts, you could assign the bass frequencies to be reproduced by them.

6.1 and 7.1

Pro Tools supports the additional mixing formats of 6.1 and 7.1, as well as 6.0 and 7.0 (should you not need the LFE channel). They are assigned exactly like all other surround formats, via the I/O Setup page (choose Setups > I/O Setup). Simply select your chosen format, such as 6.1, in the pull-down menu of the Output To Path. Always make sure to label your outputs!

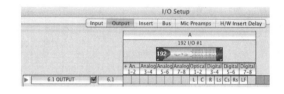

Fig. 4-20: 6.1 I/O

Fig. 4-21: 6.1 Digidesign Panner

The default surround path for 6.1, as you can see from the graphic above, is L, C, R, Ls, Cs, Rs, and LF. This adds a Cs (Center Surround) speaker icon to the standard Digidesign Surround Panner. Since there is an additional channel of audio now being routed out of the hardware interface, you'll need to connect another speaker, placed equally between the Ls (Left Surround) and Rs (Right Surround) monitors in your room. Typically, 6.1 setups are used when mixing formats such as Dolby EX and DTS-ES. (See Chapter 10, "Current Surround Formats," for additional information.)

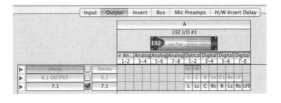

Fig. 4-20: 7.1 I/O

Fig. 4-21: 7.1 Digidesign Panner

For 7.1, assigned in the same manner as 6.1 above, the I/O setup will show
L, Lc, C, Rc, R, Ls, Rs, LFE. The Digidesign Surround Panner will reflect this as well,
with the addition of an Lc (Left Center) and Rc (Right Center) front speakers. As in
the example for 6.1, you must then connect additional speakers to your hardware
and set them up accordingly. Typically, 7.1 mixing is used with the SDDS (Sony
Dynamic Digital Sound) format for motion picture theaters, for which there is no
equivalent consumer format.

CHAPTER 5

Controlling Your Surround Mix

5

Keeping It All in Pro Tools

There are several benefits to mixing inside Pro Tools (sometimes known as keeping the mix "in the box"). First and foremost is the total recall of every parameter. In the world of surround mixing, recalls by the artist, producer, and/or record company are a daily occurrence. Minute changes (or large ones) must be made constantly, and to reset a console every time would be a nightmare.

This is especially true when dealing with the fact that surround mixes typically share information coming from five or more channels. The variables are enormous, and therefore, the need for instant total recall is almost essential. I would not want to do a surround mix on a professional level without it.

Another benefit is the ease of use of all panners and plug-ins. Imagine wanting to do a simple Front-to-Back pan and having to use up to three rotary panpots to accomplish that task. Instead, you either grab a surround panner or simply use your mouse or trackpad.

Using the Waves 360 Manager (see Chapter 9), you can bass-manage your mix without resorting to external units (although there is nothing wrong with using them). Beyond being able to tune the plug-in to your specific room, it helps you keep an eye on the overall levels of your mix as well.

By keeping it all inside of Pro Tools, there are also fewer cables involved, lessening the chance of phase issues creeping in, and reducing the hassle of tracking down a bad cable. I'm a believer in the less-is-more approach, and keeping it in the box lets me work fast when I need to. Don't forget, time is money!

Some good reasons to keep your surround mix "inside the box":

• Total automation of all parameters.

• Instant total recall for all mix changes.

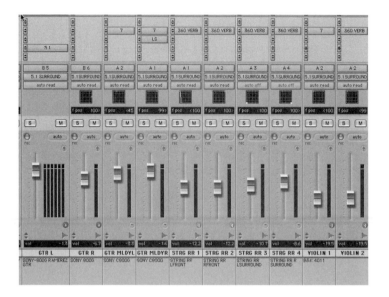

Fig. 5-1: Full Surround Mix Window

- The ability to bass-manage with a plug-in.

- Panning is incredibly easy.

- No need to hook up external equipment.

- Less worries about bad cables and phase issues.

- The ability to work faster, as time is money.

It's important to know that you don't need a surround controller in order to mix in surround sound. The fact is, all the surround controls you need are built into the Pro Tools software. As long as you have multichannel panners and six to eight channels of separate output, you're good to go. I've even mixed several multi-channel releases on my PowerBook G4 laptop—using my Pro Tools HD 192 I/O rig, a Magma expansion chassis, and the trackpad. All the 5.1 mixes done that way were bounced internally, burned to DVD, and shipped off the mastering plant for final touches and encoding.

Without question, though, having a surround controller simplifies everything, so mixing with one would certainly be my recommendation. The brand and specific type you choose is largely a matter of personal taste.

Digidesign Control Surfaces

Icon

Icon is an integrated console that users can configure to meet their individual needs, all based around a D-Control tactile work surface. The master module has a full complement of controls, including a 16-channel Fader Module (up to 80 total touch-

Fig. 5-2: Icon

sensitive, motorized faders can be added). There are 29 illuminated pushbuttons per channel strip and two bargraph meters per channel, along with eight Master section bargraph meters for comprehensive surround monitoring.

Icon supports mixes up to 24-bit/192kHz in 7.1 surround, and of course, every parameter is fully automatable. Each channel also has six touch-sensitive multi-purpose rotary encoders with 15-segment multi-color LED rings, as well as a six-character multi-color LCD display (and a scribble strip). There's a dedicated control section for dynamics and EQ plug-in editing. It's all connected to your Pro Tools system via Ethernet.

Options include digital and analog I/O, integrated remote-controlled microphone preamps, Avid picture support and machine control, plus synchronization support. With the XMON remote analog I/O monitor system (made via DB-25 connections), you can even monitor two separate eight-channel mixes as well as four stereo sources.

Pro Control

Using Pro Control is a great way to mix surround sound within Pro Tools. It connects to your TDM system using a standard 10Base-T Ethernet connection, allowing for easy networking as well. There are eight motorized, touch-sensitive 100mm DigiFaders, with 10-bit (1,024-step) resolution.

The main power of Pro Control lies not only in its multichannel output options, but in its total automation capabilities. You can control Write, Touch, Latch, and Read modes for fader levels, sends, mutes, and pans. In addition, plug-ins can be controlled by mapping them to the faders for touch-sensitive automation.

Pro Control also provides scrub/shuttle functions, transport controls, edit tool/modes, and even a trackpad. There are high-resolution LED meters, eight-character

Fig. 5-3: Pro Control

scribble strips, and illuminated buttons. Three DB-25 connectors are provided: two for monitor section inputs and one for output.

Pro Control can be expanded up to 48 faders (in banks of eight), and it supports Edit Pack (see below) for total control of multichannel mixing. When I'm mixing surround outside of my home facility, this is the unit I prefer, for its simplicity and overall functionality.

Edit Pack

This editing and surround mixing surface for Pro Control features eight high-res 40-segment meters for easy reading of your surround levels. There are two motorized, touch-sensitive DigiPanner joysticks, as well as dedicated access to pans, X/Y variable divergence controls, solos, mute, channel assigns, and LFE control. It has a two-button trackball, a color-coded QWERTY keyboard, and a 10Base-T Ethernet connection. With a Pro Control and an Edit Pack, you're seriously in the surround game.

Control 24

Control 24 is different from Pro Control in that it is more like a traditional console. It features 16 Focusrite Class A mix preamps, as well as 24 touch-sensitive faders. As you might expect, it allows for full 5.1 surround monitoring and total

Fig. 5-4: Edit Pack

Fig. 5-5: Control 24

control over all routing, recording, mixing, and editing parameters. High-resolution LED meters are also provided for comprehensive visual monitoring.

There are dedicated EQ and Dynamics switches for every channel, as well as illuminated switches for Solo, Mute, Record Arm, Automation Mode, and Channel Selects. Using the Plug-In Flip Mode, you can have touch-sensitive automation for all plug-in parameters. Overall, Control 24 packs a lot of punch for a surround producer.

Command 8

Command 8 supports TDM systems, connecting to the host computer via USB. There are eight touch-sensitive motorized faders and eight automatable rotary encoders with LED rings. A backlit LCD display handles the character display, and there's even a useful one-in/two-out MIDI interface. Command 8 can be used in conjunction with Pro Control, Control 24, and/or a Digi 002 (since it also works with LE systems).

Fig. 5-6: Command 8

Third-Party Surround Controllers

There are several other excellent controllers on the market that provide varying degrees of functionality for surround mixing. If a certain model doesn't have a surround panner, that doesn't mean you can't mix surround with it. Just hook it up to your computer and use it to control faders, plug-ins, aux sends, etc. For specific surround control over pans and outputs, simply use Pro Tools itself (unless, of course, the controller can handle that function).

Let's take a look at a few of these other control surfaces.

Motor Mix

www.digidesign.com

Motor Mix works with TDM systems, so you can use it to control certain aspects of a surround mix. It communicates with Pro Tools via MIDI I/O, and its 100mm motion-sensing faders are all motorized. Each channel features a non-detented knob for pan, EQ, aux send, and plug-in control. There's a 40x2-dot LCD display for

Fig. 5-7: Motor Mix

parameter control info, and up to four units can be linked for a small but efficient 32-channel system.

To get Motor Mix to work with Pro Tools, simply open a session, select "controllers" in the Peripherals menu, and select "HUI." Then select the number of channels you want to work with. For Pro Tools 5.X and higher, pull down the MIDI menu and choose "MIDI INPUT DEVICES." If you then click on the Motor Mix option, you will enable Pro Tools to receive its MIDI input; it's that easy.

Tascam Us-2400

www.tascam.com

This DAW controller connects to your computer using a simple USB cable, and will operate with Pro Tools under HUI mode (on both the Mac OSX and Windows XP platforms). It has 25 touch-sensitive 100mm moving faders and assignable encoders that control pan, aux level- or channel-strip functions like EQs, etc. There's a motorized master fader along with a full set of tranport controls, as well as a jog/shuttle wheel. For surround panning, there's a joystick, along with a set of fully assignable function keys.

Fig. 5-8: Tascam Us-2400

Mackie Control Universal

www.mackie.com

This control surface hooks up to Pro Tools via HUI control, and offers 100mm Penny + Giles optical touch-sensitive faders, full meter display with track names and parameters, a backlit LCD, and V-Pots for plug-in and effect control (as well as panning). You can easily add more channels with the optional Control Extenders.

Fig. 5-9: Mackie Control Universal

External Console Mixing

Some engineers and/or producers prefer to mix surround sound on external consoles. Typically, you would take the individual outputs from Pro Tools and send them to a console on a channel-by-channel basis. Once the signals are routed to the board, panning, EQ, compression, and overall mix levels can be adjusted accordingly.

Some engineers opt to combine elements of Pro Tools' internal processing and external mixing, sending only selected channels to a console. Again, there is no right or wrong method; it becomes an issue of personal style. While this method does require more individual I/Os, it allows those who enjoy console mixing the opportunity to get the sound they are seeking from the board, be it analog or digital.

Some digital consoles are now offering direct Pro Tools software control. For example, SSL's AWS 900 console features HUI compatibility, allowing for such things as transport control, fader movements, plug-in control, and parameter access. It features 5.1 outputs, allowing individual channel control of your surround mix. Mackie's dXb consoles feature Mackie Control Universal mode for Pro Tools control, and Yamaha's O2R96 and DM2000 feature integrated DAW control as well.

Pro Tools has become such a standard medium that you can expect that most digital console manufacturers will offer Pro Tools control; if it isn't already implemented, then you can expect it in the near future.

External Surround Monitor Control

Not all multichannel monitor controllers are actually control surfaces. Some, like the one I use on my home surround setup (the Grace Design m906), have no faders (or meters) on them. They are simply external "audio throughputs" for the monitoring of surround-sound signal. I happen to like this type of unit for its direct digital signal path from Pro Tools and the pristine audio clarity that it provides.

The units below offer an excellent way to monitor your surround mixes:

- Tascam DS-M7.1 (www.tascam.com)

- SPL Model 2380 (www.spl-usa.com)

- MultiMax EX (www.martinsound.com)

- EMM Labs Switchmaster Quartet (www.emmlabs.com)

- Kurzweil KSP8 w/mLan card (www.kurzweil.com)

- Grace Design m906 (www.gracedesign.com)

- Adgil Director (www.sascom.com)

- Studio Technologies StudioComm Model 78/Model 79 (www.studiotechnologies.com)

To give you an idea of what it does and why I use it at home, below is an excerpt from an article I recently wrote about the Grace m906.

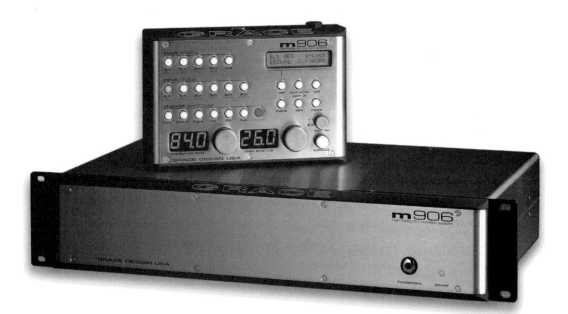

Figu. 5-10: Front of Grace M906

Since I'm a work-at-home studio type, this unit is perfect for my setup. I run a Pro Tools HD3/Accel setup with a 192 I/O into a dual 2GHz G5 computer, along with a full 5.1 monitoring setup, an Oxygen 8 keyboard, and a stack of high-quality preamps. All of my reverbs, compressors, and soft synths are in the computer—the rest now sit in the closet for when I need them. The system is clean, crisp, powerful, and totally automated. For quick setup, I simply plug the m906 digitally into the 192 I/O via optical cable. The audio path is then directly distributed to my speakers through the mainframe, and the remote control unit sits on my desktop.

One of the first things I liked about this unit was its solid feel. The mainframe unit comes with analog and digital I/O and a 1/2 RU external power supply, 6-pin XLR DC power cable, and a remote control unit with 25' remote cable. Setup and plug-in are painless, but you should certainly read through the comprehensive I/O option list. I started with a simple ADAT optical cable for single-cable, eight-channel input up to 48kHz. I plugged my CD player into the S/PDIF input, and my universal (DVD/SA-CD) player into the six unbalanced (–10dBV) inputs. I then ran the optical output of my G5 into the m906. Also, I can easily hook up another set (or two!) of monitors.

I had a good-quality DB25 digital cable built so I could use the AES3 multi-channel input for full multichannel resolutions up to 192kHz. The m906 can accept analog or digital inputs, and can be referenced to AES3, ADAT, S/PDIF, and TOSLINK digital clock. There is also the option to hook up external Word or SuperClock if you choose. Interestingly, the m906 uses a technology Grace Design calls s-Lock PLL (Phase Lock Loop). PLL is automatically applied once the unit detects the incoming clock source, providing a highly stable, ultra-low-jitter clock to run the unit's DACs.

Aside from all the I/O options (check out the picture to see them all), there are two headphone outs: one on the remote and one on the mainframe. A separate stepped rotary encoder on the remote dials up the volume in well-lit 0.5dB increments, allowing me to monitor every mix on a record at exactly the same volume. It also helps that the 906's headphone amplifier is based on the Grace 901 reference headphone amp, except that this one lets me listen to signals of up to 192kHz. In my first headphone experience, I found some background noise in my mix I had never heard before, thanks to the quality of not only the amplifier, but also the unit's converters. It was a "wow" moment, literally.

Grace also thoughtfully included a fixed-level 5.1 DAC output, fed directly from whatever is selected as your current digital source. Essentially, you can route a direct digital surround mix to a multichannel recorder, set at 0dB as the default. On that note, the m906 has many hidden features. Apart from the LCD screen, headphone and volume knobs, digital meters, channel solo/mutes, and input selectors (analog and digital), there is also a calibration mode. This can be used for such things as input source offsets, individual 5.1 speaker output levels, and fixed DAC output level and talkback/48v phantom settings. Talkback? Yes, there is even an XLR input for this, which is essentially a single channel from a Grace 801R preamp; there's even an included footswitch jack for external operation, should you opt not to press the talkback button on the remote.

I grew up with a father who always paid a little extra for things that were well made, would last for years, and got the job done efficiently. That mantra applies to how I buy studio gear as well. The Grace Design m906 is worth the investment and I'm now a very satisfied customer. To me, it's not only a supreme high-quality 5.1 monitor controller, it's now the nerve center of my entire studio.

Bass Management Controllers

Several companies offer external bass management controllers. Like a component stereo system, sometimes you must combine several separate pieces to create a complete surround monitoring setup. Considering how important bass management is when mixing surround, I certainly suggest considering a product like this, if you don't already have a way to handle it. Here are a couple of products to check out:

Managermax

www.martinsound.com

Designed in conjunction with Tomlinson Holman and the TMH Corporation, ManagerMax has five continuously adjustable 2nd-order highpass filters and a six-position 4th-order lowpass filter for redirection of low frequencies. The LFE filter is defeatable, and features a brick-wall filter emulating surround decoders. The redirected LFE and bass channel are then summed for easy setup. Check out the company's website for a nice line of additional useful surround products.

Blue Sky Bmc

www.abluesky.com

This unit offers full bass management and remote multi-channel volume control in a nice, small package. There are individual output modes and master calibration/ level controls, LFE level adjustment at 0dB or +10dB, and reference and mute controls. Of course, there are 5.1 channels of bass management, +24dBu fully balanced XLR I/Os, and a full-function remote control.

Multichannel Mixing Concepts

6

Mixing the Center Channel

What goes into the Center channel is an often-debated and ever-controversial subject among those who produce surround recordings. Many engineers use the Center channel to "lock in" the image of a vocal, kick drum, snare drum, and bass guitar, while also mixing some of each into the front Left and Right channels. That's typically done in case a consumer has no Center speaker.

Some engineers don't use the Center channel at all, but the consumer may feel slighted or confused if there is nothing there on playback! Since much of the music I mix has vocals, I'll use the Center channel to create a strong mono image, though

Fig. 6-1: Center channel from Digi panner

still relying on the Left and Right speakers to carry most of the actual signal. I also use the Center in the same fashion with the kick, snare, hats, and bass (if there are any)—again relying on the rest of the speakers to carry the mix. The Center should simply help you present a stronger image in the front of your mix than you could achieve with plain old stereo.

Another technique I use for Center channel imaging is to utilize the power of the surrounds. Taking the previously mentioned vocal as an example, I would create a Left Surround/Right Surround send in Pro Tools' I/O setup and use it sparingly. This will "pull" the vocal outside of the front speakers, especially off the Center channel. Therefore, with divergence, there will be some vocal in every channel, including the surrounds.

You can also create a stereo delay on a stereo aux send and pan it to the Left Surround/Right Surround speakers. Then, as you gradually increase the send from that mono vocal, the image will increasingly envelop you. If you dampen the frequency of the delay's returns, the overall effect becomes less noticeable, creating a nice sense of vocal space, especially when the rest of the mix gets added in. This technique can be applied to any instrument; I often treat guitars and snares the same way.

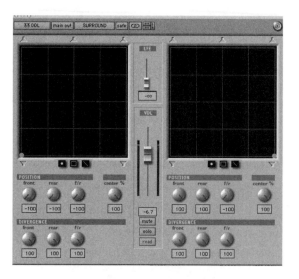

Fig. 6-2: Stereo delay, panned to the rear channels

A nice trick I've learned is to send just enough to the surrounds so that you can actually hear the effect, then back it down slightly until you don't notice it. If you mute the effect, you'll hear a difference. This technique adds a nice sense of depth using the surround field.

Center Percentage on Surround Panners

Don't forget to experiment with the Center % (Percentage) amount on the Pro Tools and Waves surround panners. By default, the Pro Tools panner is set at 100%, which is not always good for mixing.

When I convert a stereo mix into multichannel by applying surround panners to a group of tracks, the first thing I do to each of them is adjust that Center percentage. I don't want them set to that high a percentage of Center, unless I'm going for a certain effect. It forces too much information out of the Center channel, and as I've mentioned before, who knows how a consumer will have their system set up. It's best to be safe and let several speakers carry an image, especially relying on the front Left/Rights.

For film production, having dialog in the Center channel alone makes sense— hence a 100% setting. But for music applications, having a vocal or main melodic instrument there at 100% may not be appropriate. As you reduce the Center Percentage value, the image will broaden itself out to each adjacent channel.

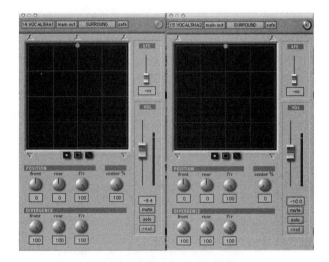

Fig. 6-3: 100% Center, 0% Center

When the setting is at 0, you create what is called a "phantom" center image. The front Left and Right channels reproduce enough of an audio signal to make it sound like the image is projecting from the center. This phantom center is also the essence of stereo mixing, and one of the reasons why surround sound appeals to so many producers. You no longer have to rely on those Left and Right speakers alone to create a center image; you've got another channel to do so. So use it wisely, carefully mixing in elements to provide a nice, wide soundfield around the listener.

Approaches to the LFE

The use of the LFE (.1 channel) is another hot topic. Consumers seem to love a thundering subwoofer, as I do myself, and engineers have many options to work with. Again, this is down to the preference of the production team. When working with LFE information, I can't stress enough how important it is to check your mixes with bass management. Remember that frequencies around 100Hz and lower will often be routed from all speakers to the subwoofer during consumer playback!

Here's something to think about: Let's say you had a kick drum with either a Digidesign or Waves surround panner on it. On the Digi panner there is an LFE slider; the equivalent on the Waves panner is the Send to LFE value box.

If that kick drum has lots of information around 80Hz and you do *not* send any low-frequency information from it to the LFE channel, most receivers' bass management functions would route that 80Hz to the subwoofer for playback anyway. Don't forget, very few home theater surround speakers can handle that frequency (I'm trying to drill this fact into your heads).

Fig. 6-4: Waves panner showing send to LFE

If, however, you *do* route some kick information to the LFE channel, the consumer will hear that 80Hz frequency through both the LFE channel that you created *and* via bass management. As a result, it would probably make your mix quite muddy, considering there are lots of other low frequencies in a kick, not to mention any other instruments in your mix in that frequency range. Therein again lies the value of checking your mix with bass management, and being very careful about what LFE information you create in a mix.

The more surround projects I mix, the less I find myself using the LFE send. Often, I let bass management handle the entire low end in my mix. Sometimes, though, a little LFE send can really pump up the bottom of a mix. Again, experience can help you with this.

To add specific LFE information to a mix you can either use the LFE slider on the appropriate panner or output window, or create an LFE sub-path in the I/O setup and route it discretely. Note that there is no filtering applied directly to an LFE signal in Pro Tools.

Check Your Mixes

When mixing at Gizmo Studios in New York, I often send my mix digitally into a consumer receiver setup in the next room, using the studio's Dolby or DTS hardware encoders. This lets me check the overall levels, how bass management is reacting to the mix, if the Center channel is too hot, and whether or not there is enough surround information. Note that this is an imperfect method, because some people set their subwoofer crossovers at 80Hz, some at 100Hz, and some at up to 120Hz. However, it is a good way to get an idea of how your mix translates. The objective of any surround sound mixing engineer is to enable the consumer to feel the low end properly upon playback in their home theater—which is certainly not a simple task. Checking your mixes as you go along can help dramatically.

Center Percentage

Proper use of center percentage is a remarkably useful tool when carving out a good multichannel mix. If you listen to the first few audio examples of the included DVD, you will hear how different a vocal can sound when carefully utilizing center percentage with the front Left, Center and Right channels.

Remember that by default, Pro Tools surround panners are set at 100% Center. Make sure to go through each channel in your mix and adjust this accordingly.

Mixing to Picture

Many multichannel projects, especially those for live concert DVD-videos or concert broadcasts, involve mixing to picture. In these kinds of situations, you'll be watching video while mixing. This has many useful applications, such as following the action onscreen with fader or pan movements, creating specific surround effects, or *not* increasing a vocal level when a performer is off microphone, thus making the mix sound a bit unreal. Of course, the film world always mixes to picture, and they have their own set of rules for dialog, effects, Foley, etc. But the principles are the same: Follow the action onscreen and make your mix moves accordingly.

There are several ways that Pro Tools users can mix surround to picture. One of the more common methods, which is actually one of the simplest to work with, is to use QuickTime movies.

QuickTime

The integration of QuickTime movies within Pro Tools is an important and powerful feature. Not only is this the easiest and quickest way to score to picture, but you don't need any additional hardware to have frame-accurate video synchronization with your audio. The applications I've scored in Pro Tools include concert videos, TV commercials, industrials, web programs, movie trailers, and video game elements.

Typically, when scoring to a QuickTime movie within Pro Tools, I have the content creators deliver me a 640 x 480 (pixel) full-frame digital movie. This is also useful if you have a second monitor to view full-screen video on. If they are sending me a spot over the web, or when I want to just watch it in the Movie window, I have them encode the QuickTime file at 320 x 240. Often, I request that the video creators include what's called a "window burn," or "burn in window." This is simply a visual representation of SMPTE timecode in the video window, usually in a black box at the bottom. It allows for easy frame-accurate spotting of audio, especially when following a cue sheet.

The larger-pixel movies have better resolution and are easier to score to, but they may tax your system resources a bit more. The overall quality of Pro Tools movie playback will vary based upon your computer speed, hard drive speed, quality of the actual encode, and size of the movie itself. For 25–30 frames-per-second full-screen video playback, you'll need a Digidesign-approved video capture and playback card.

Here's how you import a QuickTime movie into Pro Tools:

1. Create a new Pro Tools session or open an existing one.

2. Make sure the timecode settings of your session match the QuickTime movie you are going to import. This is vital, since you need to watch the video in sync. Several times I've lost sync and when I've poked around to find out why, I've noticed that the settings in my session didn't match the movie.

3. Choose Movie > Import Movie.

4. Navigate to the movie and then click Open. Pro Tools will import the movie, placing the first frame automatically at the start time of your session.

5. If the QuickTime movie you've chosen has audio with it, you can import that as well. Choose Movie > Import Audio From Current Movie. A QuickTime Track Import window will appear, showing you the audio track selected. Choose OK, and the audio will appear on a track beginning exactly where the movie starts. Save your session, press Play, and you should be locked and loaded.

The Movie Track

After following that procedure, you'll notice two new things: a floating Movie window is on the screen and the QuickTime movie now has its own Movie track in the Edit window. Also, there are probably frames of video showing in the timeline. This happens because Pro Tools defaults the Movie track to Key Frames mode. You can show more or less detail of the movie by zooming in or out in the Edit window. This is very useful for super-accurate spotting, but it uses up quite a bit of your computer's CPU power.

I suggest switching the Movie track to Block mode; it's far less processor-intensive and allows you to move the track around just like audio. I always move this new track to the top of the Edit window, just to keep things organized. Note that you can't edit this Movie track within the Pro Tools application, however. You can also set the movie playback priority in the Movie menu. Medium Priority Playback works quite well on most of today's fast computers, but you can also choose High Priority Playback at the expense of some onscreen graphic tasks. I also suggest that you capture and play back QuickTime video on a separate drive than your Pro Tools audio drive. Most of the applications I've scored have been short in duration, and it's been fine to keep them on the same drive, but for longer movies, using a separate drive is a good idea.

Pro Tools offers scrubbing of the Movie track, using the Scrubber tool. However, by scrubbing directly on the Movie track, the movie will scrub with no audio playback. If you scrub on the audio itself, the movie will scrub along with it. You can also hold down the Command key during scrub for precise movements.

- QuickTime is not just a media player; it's multimedia technology architecture.

- Every day, more than 300,000 people download QuickTime to view news, entertainment, movies, and virtual reality content on the web.

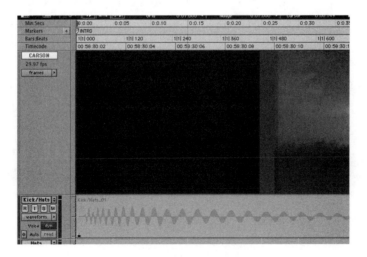

Fig. 6-5: Movie track key frames

- Always try to use the fastest computer possible for smoother movie playback.

- QuickTime supports MPEG, AVI, Sorenson, Cinepak, Flash, and DV.

- Mac owners have it already installed. Just do a Find (Command-F) if you don't see it.

- PC owners have to install it. Note that Windows Media Player (.WMV) documents are not Pro Tools compatible.

- Be sure to always download the latest version. www.apple.com is a great place to check for updates/downloads.

- Digidesign's Sync I/O will allow for the display of a timecode burn-in window, which can be turned on or off.

It's often recommended to keep DV (digital video) files either on a separate drive or on your computer's drive. This is especially true when using long video clips, FireWire drives, and/or sessions that have a lot of tracks. On occasion, I've gotten this message on my Pro Tools screen: *"DAE can't get audio from the disk(s) fast enough. Your disk may be too slow or too fragmented. A FireWire disk could be having trouble due to the extra FireWire bandwidth or CPU load (−9073)."* This is often referred to as a −9073 error message amongst Digi friends. The few times I did get that message when scoring to picture, I simply moved the video elements to a separate FireWire drive and the problem went away.

Other Methods of Syncing Video to Pro Tools

Gallery's Virtual VTR is another option for scoring to picture using QuickTime. You need a second Mac computer to run it on, but it takes the CPU and processing burden of running video off your main system. Working much like a stand-alone VTR, it's controlled either by MIDI or via 9-pin machine control. With a G4 and OSX, for example, you can score to picture without any dedicated video hardware. It chases timecode using a SMPTE-to-MTC converter, and it can also act as a timecode master when using an external timecode generator. For more information check out their website (www.virtualvtr.com).

Using Digidesign's SYNC I/O (or any other compatible video sync), you can also lock your Pro Tools setup to an external video tape recorder (VTR). Locking picture via 9-pin control, you can use Pro Tools to shuttle the video deck by selecting Machine from the Transport dropdown menu on the Transport control. Timecode numbers can be punched in for exact locations, and Pro Tools can work as either a SMPTE slave or as the transport master. Read your manual for further specifics on video synchronization.

Case Study: Reverse Mixing to Picture

Recently, I had the pleasure of mixing seven tracks from an upcoming DVD for the American Drummers Achievement Awards honoring Steve Gadd. The event, presented by the Avedis Zildjian cymbal company, featured a world-class band that included Michael Landau on guitar, Jimmy Johnson on bass, and Larry Goldings on keyboards, along with guest appearances by Will Lee on vocals and Tom Scott on sax. Vinnie Colaiuta and Rick Marotta performed alternately and together on drums, and the music selection included songs from Gadd's career. The evening closed with a performance by Gadd, James Taylor, and the band. For this particular project, the producers decided to do the surround mix from the perspective of the drummer's seat. The live recording, done by engineer Sean McClintock, included not only close and overhead drum mics for every kit, but stereo audience mics, balcony mics, and a Soundfield mic onstage (stereo only), in addition to instruments and vocals.

Since the perspective is actually reversed from a typical live concert, the audience mics were panned in the front Left/Right speakers instead of the surrounds. The balcony mics were used in front as well, but kept quite low, as they had a lot of slapback. Since it was a mix-to-picture situation, I could visually see where each drum was positioned, allowing me to pan accordingly in the (now reversed) surround field. The overheads were placed almost in the middle between the front Left/Right and Left/Right Surrounds, but just slightly towards the front of the stage. (Placing them right in the middle of the front/back speakers can be dangerous, as consumers don't always have their room set up correctly!) The Soundfield microphone was placed almost in the same spot, but slightly back to create some extra ambience. The rest of the various kits and the kick, snare, hat, and tom mics were pulled back from the front speakers, following the natural arc of each drum set.

The overall effect is very exciting to hear and watch, and could never be duplicated with stereo. Distributed by Hudson Music, the DVD has other additional features, but including surround tracks like this increases the project's overall value. It's also nice that 100% of Zildjian's net proceeds from the sale of this disc are contributed to scholarships at the Berklee College of Music.

Preparing Your Elements

Gizmo Audio/Video in New York City is where I do most of my surround mixing. Owned by industry veterans Gary Moscato and Brian Mackewich, they foresaw the value of multichannel production for music, commercial, DVD, HD, and industrial releases several years ago, investing in both the knowledge and equipment to do so. I thought it would be interesting for readers to have Brian answer some questions on how he prepares both audio and video elements for a multichannel mix.

Fig. 6-6: Brian Mackewich in Gizmo

Q: What process do you typically go through to "tune the room" for a surround session?

A: This is possibly the most important aspect of surround, excluding bass management. There are several steps. Make sure that your Pro Tools rig is calibrated before you start calibrating the room itself. Otherwise, you will be wasting your time. We use the Waves 360 Bundle to make the task much easier, as the calibration instructions that come with it are spot on.

Q: The studio has both software and hardware encoders for surround. How do you use each one?

A: The hardware encoders work with a PC-based software package from Dolby or DTS. It works and sounds great, but the software is a little cranky. You feed audio and TC [timecode] into the units and the resulting bitstream file is recorded to disc on the PC. If you are encoding for Pro Logic, Dolby Digital, or Dolby E, the encoded audio may be laid back to videotape masters. At Gizmo, we usually import AC-3 directly into our DVD authoring system.

The software encoders are like AudioSuite plug-ins. If you are encoding directly from Pro Tools–based sources, this is an incredibly effective way to get the job done. You select a channel layout that matches your six-channel mix elements and the desired format. Then you modify all of the parameter settings based on the project's delivery specs. Hit Encode and go get a cup of coffee. Apple A-pack works very well, depending on your needs. We also use the decoders to check the mixes as we go. It is a good precaution. You can spot trouble before you get in too deep.

Q: How do you check the surround mixes once they are encoded?

A: You can check the encode by importing it back into Pro Tools, since it's an AES bitstream. Just patch the outputs into a pro or consumer decoder and check the mix! We have a consumer playback system set up in our Foley room to check mixes on as well. In the case of hardware encoding, you can use the supplied software player on the PC and feed the output into your decoder to check for proper playback.

Q: How do you usually sync picture elements to audio for surround mix-to-picture situations?

A: We use a variety of methods and gear. The most common is using the Digidesign SYNC I/O. It uses 9-pin RS-232 control and timecode from a deck, and it will slave Pro Tools to the deck. You can also use machine control.

Another option is digital picture. You can use an Aurora Fuse or Pipe card (depending on what OS you are running), which sits in one of the PCI slots of your computer. You simply import a QT [QuickTime movie] and sync it up to the timecode. I like to capture the QT with visual code burned in, so that you know when you are in sync. The major drawback of this choice is that importing video into Pro Tools puts a great deal of strain on the OS and occasionally bogs it down. It works best when the clips are short and/or encoded at moderate resolutions. There are several digital sync-to-pic boxes that use 9-pin control and are random access.

Q: For the David Bowie Ziggy Stardust Live *DVD, there was no timecode present on the audio masters. How did you sync the audio elements to the video on that project?*

A: This was old school and hi-tech mixed together. The masters were sent over from David Bowie's vault. It was great—about 30 reels of two-inch tape showed up from the annals of rock history. We went through the notes and determined which reels were actually needed. We then transferred the discrete tracks to Pro Tools using extreme-high-quality converters. Roy Thomas Baker did the field recordings, and they sounded extremely good to begin with.

However, the tapes had no TC on them, as this was not yet a common practice in film mixing and acquisition in 1973. They did print a 60Hz pilot tone or "crystal sync" on track 16. During the transfer, we had to resolve the two-inch machine to this frequency to assure that the speed was exact. This was the only chance we had of being able to sync the audio to the newly restored picture.

That was a very difficult part of the project. Once all the tracks were in Pro Tools, we then had to manually place sound to picture, making adjustments for each reel of tape. Sometimes, we adjusted from song to song, and Pro Tools had to be set for pull-down. We were very fortunate that everything locked and stayed in sync. It was very important, as this project was being released in both DVD and for a limited theatrical run.

Downmixing

Downmixing is what happens when a multichannel mix is reproduced in stereo. On most projects, it is always best to include a separate stereo mix, for those consumers without surround playback. Sometimes, though, the 5.1 channel downmix is the only option.

When creating a multichannel mix, it's important to always check your downmix. The Waves 360 Manager has options that allow you to listen to playback of your mix in stereo and mono with a single mouse click. Remember, though, this is just a simple way of hearing what it may sound like to a consumer at home.

When encoding material for Dolby Digital, WMA9, or MLP playback, there are Metadata settings involved, which are referred to as "downmix coefficients." They allow you, during encoding, to choose how stereo DVD players mix down the surround sound. There are conflicting opinions as to how to set these coefficients. (Imagine that!)

Here are some typical downmix settings that usually reproduce fairly well in stereo:

- Left Front: −3dB

- Right Front: −3dB

- Center: −6dB

- Left Surround: −6dB

- Right Surround: −6dB

- LFE: −6dB or OFF

It's important to remember that downmixing from surround creates additional amplitude in the resulting stereo mix. In a 5.1 mix, for example, the surround Left and Right, Center, and LFE (which is sometimes just left out) must be summed into stereo with the front Left and Right channels. This could potentially create a digital overload, and we all know how that sounds. (Terrible!)

Note that SA-CD and DTS provide no downmix options (again, another reason to always include a stereo mix when possible). When authoring a project, you could choose to have the stereo mix become the default option, but confused consumers may not know how to get the surround! This is a choice of the project producer or production team. *Always check your downmix!*

Upmixing

The term "upmixing" is used when a multichannel mix is created from a stereo or mono source and not from a multitrack master. There are several ways this can be accomplished. First, there are software programs that can do so, such as Lexicon's Logic7 package in their 960L Processor or TC Electronic's Unwrap in their System 6000.

You can also use your Pro Tools software to create an upmix, by combining spaced panning, delays, and reverbs. Another method that has been used is to actually play back a mix into a live room, and use surround microphones to record the sound. I know of one instance where a mono recording was upmixed into full surround using this technique.

It's important to note that upmixing cannot create a discrete multichannel surround mix. It can create a "surround experience," but, as you might expect, it's usually not nearly as effective as working from a multitrack master. Upmixing is effective when the original multitrack recordings are not available or may have been damaged.

Case Study: Bit Budgeting & DVD Production

Currently the Director of NBC New Media in New York, David Ondrick is an accomplished new media developer and musician who has produced music, websites, and DVD/CD titles for many years. He has authored and managed numerous internal and commercially released titles while at NBC. To learn more about projects David has worked on, check out www.nbcnewmedia.com or www.duplexity.com.

Below is a useful case study he developed on the concept of "bit budgeting" and its overall effect on several multichannel DVD projects.

Bit Budgeting & DVD Production

Bit budgeting is a very important part of any DVD production. It is an extremely valuable planning tool for the DVD producer, used to calculate bit rates for the project's assets. It is also a way to raise red flags early in the production process. Sometimes after doing a bit budget, the producer will find that there may not be enough room on the disc to fit everything the client wants at a quality level they expect from the DVD (such as a DTS surround mix along with a Dolby Digital, etc.). It's much better to know these details early on in the project than to have the last-minute nightmares of missing your client's deadlines and expectations.

As an audio professional who is interested mainly in the mixing aspect of the production process, you may look at this section and wonder why it has any relevance to you. I would say that you should take the time to read this section of the book as it will provide insights into the DVD creation process, and will oftentimes determine the types of tweaks you might have to do to your mixes as an audio subcontractor in a DVD production. While you may never actually use the formulas and concepts outlined here, having a general knowledge will make you a more valuable member of any DVD production team.

What Is It?

So what is bit budgeting? It is the DVD producer's process of calculating target bit rates for all of the various assets that the client has requested to be included in the project. The task at hand is to make sure that the sum of all of the bit rates for the assets on your disc doesn't exceed the physical space on the disc or the maximum one-time throughput of the DVD spec, which is 9.8 Mbits/second (Megabits per second, or Mbps). The idea is to plan ahead with a list of all the disc's contents so that you don't have expensive re-encodes and additional work at the end of the project—which will ultimately translate into missed deadlines and unsatisfied customers. So let's break down the various aspects of the actual DVD specification and see how they relate to the bit-budgeting process.

DVD Basics—The Physical Disc

Currently there are four types of physical discs on the DVD market. At the time of the writing of this book, there are other higher-density formats in the works, which will be discussed at the end of this chapter. The four types of discs are broken down by the amount of data that they hold. All discs are the same physical size, but their capacity is different. The table below outlines the capacity in GB for each disc type, the Mbits (determined by multiplying by eight), and the "real world" capacity with 4% headroom buffer. We will use these real world numbers later on as we begin to calculate the formulas for the bit budget.

Disc Name	Disc Capacity (GB)	Disc Capacity (Mbits)	Disc Capacity with 4% Headroom (Mbits)
DVD-5: single side, single layer	4.7 GB	37,600 Mbits	36,096 Mbits
DVD-9: single side, dual layer	8.5 GB	68,000 Mbits	65,280 Mbits
DVD-10: double side, single layer	9.4 GB	75,200 Mbits	72,192 Mbits
DVD-18: double side, double layer	17 GB	136,000 Mbits	130,560 Mbits

Table 6.1: Physical disc space for types of DVDs commercially available today

DVD Basics: The Data Throughput

The maximum data throughput of the DVD disc is 9.8 Mbps. What does this mean? If we think of the DVD throughput as a pipe, it is easier to visualize what is going on with data throughput. The pipe connects the material on the disc to the processor, which decodes and presents the material to the screen. The size of the pipe is fixed; that is, the diameter of the pipe is 9.8 Mbps. If you think of the data going through the pipe as water, then it is easy to understand that there is only so much water that can go through the pipe in any given second. Anything more will either spill out or have to wait for its turn to go through.

In the case of DVD, if you exceed the maximum throughput, the disc will generally not even verify or format in the authoring stage. If you get too close to the maximum throughput of 9.8 Mbps, you tend to see things like freeze frames or skip frames in video, or sometimes you will experience audio dropouts. The information that cannot pass through the pipe is skipped. So imagine that you have spent weeks on the encoding of all of your assets without doing a preliminary bit budget. You will arrive at the authoring stage of the production, most likely close to the deadline, and the disc won't work because the software will tell you that the maximum bit rate for the DVD spec has been exceeded.

Fig. 6.7 shows the basic throughput pipe. Your job is to figure out how to manage the bit rates of your assets in that pipe so that you maximize the quality without exceeding the limits of the DVD spec. This is what the bit budgeting process enables you to do.

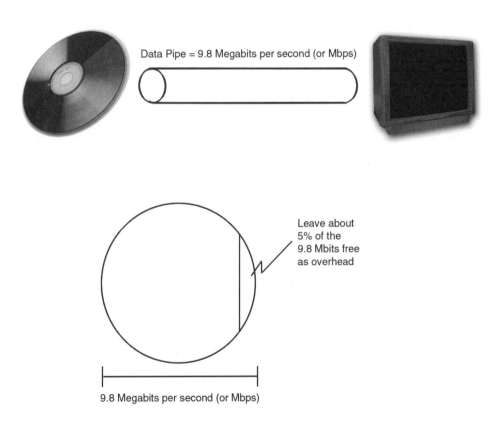

Data Pipe = 9.8 Megabits per second (or Mbps)

Leave about 5% of the 9.8 Mbits free as overhead

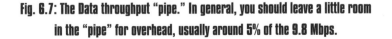

9.8 Megabits per second (or Mbps)

Fig. 6.7: The Data throughput "pipe." In general, you should leave a little room in the "pipe" for overhead, usually around 5% of the 9.8 Mbps.

Audio Assets: Typical Industry Standards for DVD Projects

As an audio professional, you have probably read or heard some of the competing standards for use with DVD. Table 6.2 outlines the basic compression schemes used for most DVDs on the market and then breaks the codecs down with the most typical bit rates used in DVD production. These numbers will be used in the next section, when we tie together all of the data in Tables 6.1, 6.2, and 6.3 to calculate our bit budget for some sample projects.

Codec Name	Channels	Typical Bit Rates
Dolby Digital	2	.192 Mbps or .384 Mbps
Dolby AC-3—5.1	6	.384 Mbps or .448 Mbps
MPEG 2 Audio	2	Up to .528 Mbps
DTS	6	.768 Mbps or 1.5 Mbps
PCM (uncompressed)	2	1.5 Mbps

Table 6.2: Typical audio bit rate requirements for industry standard DVD productions*

*Note: There are many other bit rate settings available with audio encoders like Sonic Solutions Encoder or Apple's A-Pak Encoder, but the bit rates outlined above seem to be the most typical for your standard DVDs.

Other Assets: The Subpicture Streams

You may think of the DVD as carrying only video and audio information, but there is another aspect that must be included while adding up the assets in your disc. Although this "subpicture" information is a remarkably small portion of the data throughput and physical disc space, without careful consideration, it often creates giant headaches when not accounted for properly.

Subpicture data on the DVD includes information like menu overlays, subtitles, or subpictures themselves, like navigation overlays. The subpictures are generally TIFF files or text files that are converted to MPEG streams during the authoring process and are elements that are laid over another MPEG stream.

Name of Subpicture	Bandwidth
Subpictures, Overlays, Subtitles	.040 Mbps

Table 6.3: Bandwidth for subpicture streams

Bit Budgeting Basics: The Formulas You Need to Know

There are three formulas that are used to calculate the various bit rates for your project. The most important thing to do is to get the final asset list signed off by your client. Find out exactly what the client is expecting the DVD to contain; i.e., the number of minutes of video, types of audio streams, number of menus, number of motion menus, number of subtitles, etc. I often do a complete navigation map before attempting the bit budget so there are fewer surprises later on in the production.

Here are the basic formulas you will use, followed by two "real world" examples and then a discussion about what the numbers mean.

Bit Budget Formula #1:

MAX Video Only Encode Bit Rate = 9.8 Mbps–(Audio Streams + Subpictures)

This formula tells you the highest bit rate allowed during the point on the disc with the most tracks. You can have a different max for the menu portion of the disc and the main content portion. You will use this number if you encode your video at variable bit rate (VBR) as your absolute highest bit rate before filling the pipe.

Bit Budget Formula #2:

Average Encoding Rate =
(Disc Type Total Mbits) divided by [(# of min. of video) x 60 sec.]

This formula makes sure your encoded video doesn't fill up the physical space on the disc, so the number of minutes of video should include video used in the menus as well.

You will use this number in Formula #3 to calculate the target bit rate for your video. Disc type total Mbits comes from the 4% headroom column in Table 6.1.

Bit Budget Formula #3:

Video Only Target Bit Rate =
(Average Encoding Rate)–(Audio Streams + Subpictures)

This formula tells you the target bit rate you need to achieve the best quality possible on your disc with all of the other assets you want to include. This is the number that will be the best gauge as to whether everything the client wants will fit on the type of delivery disc they have requested.

By this point you are probably saying, "What the heck is he talking about!" So let's go ahead and work through some real-world examples that will help clear things up.

Example 1: Concert DVD

The client has requested a DVD with the following specifications: (Remember, we have most likely laid out a navigation map to make sure *all* assets have been identified beforehand!)

- (1) Single video stream consisting of 1 hour 48 minutes of pre-edited concert footage. Footage is fast moving with lots of cuts and movement.

- (1) AC-3 surround 5.1 channel mix @ .384 Mbps

- (1) PCM uncompressed stereo mixdown @ 1.5 Mbps

- (1) Lyrics subtitle track

- (1) Menu with 30-second video loop and one menu subpicture overlay and (1) PCM audio loop.

The client has requested that the disc be delivered as a DVD-5 to match other products already released in the series.

Let's run the numbers and see what we come up with . . . .

Bit Budget Formula #1:

MAX Video Only Encode Bit Rate = 9.8 Mbps–(Audio Streams + Subpictures)

MAX Video Only Encode Bit Rate = 9.8 Mbps–[(.384 Mbps (AC3) + 1.5 Mbps PCM) + .040 Mbps (lyrics)]

MAX Video Only Encode Bit Rate = 9.8 Mbps–1.924 Mbps

MAX Video Only Encode Bit Rate = 7.87 Mbps

Bit Budget Formula #2:

Average Encoding Rate =

Disc Type Total Mbits divided by [(# of min. of video) x 60 sec.]

Average Encoding Rate = [36,096 Mbits (DVD-5) divided by [(108 minutes (video) + 30 sec. (menu loop)) x 60]

Average Encoding Rate = 36,096 divided by 6,510

Average Encoding Rate = 5.54 Mbps

Bit Budget Formula #3:

Video Only Target Bit Rate =

(Average Encoding Rate)–(Audio Streams + Subpictures)

Video Only Target Bit Rate = 5.54 Mbps – [(.384 Mbps (AC3) +1.5 Mbps (PCM) + .040 Mbps (lyrics)]

Video Only Target Bit Rate = 3.616 Mbps

Example 1 Discussion:

So what does it all mean? Let's take a look at what we've got.

Here is what we calculated:

1. *MAX Video Encode Bit Rate = 7.87 Mbps*

2. *AVG. Video Encode Rate = 5.54 Mbps*

3. *Video Only Target Bit Rate = 3.616 Mbps*

These numbers look good. As noted in the client specs, the footage has a lot of cuts and a lot of fast moving action. This type of footage tends to drive up the bit rates of the encoded video, because the MPEG-2 encoder has to use more key frames (I-frames) to create the files. More key frames, or complete frames, means more data throughput. Assuming we are using variable bit rate encoding, which allows us to raise or lower the bit rate based on the scene we are looking at, it appears we have plenty of headroom at 7.87 Mbps for the spots with the most action, and we should be able to achieve our average of 5.54 Mbps with a target of 3.616 Mbps. So in this scenario, the assets will easily fit on the DVD-5 disc and we will have some room to play with higher bit rates if there are problem sections in the video with tons of cuts and motion. You might even be able to play around with a higher bit rate on the AC-3. Instead of .384 Mbps, run the numbers with a .768 Mbps AC-3 stream and see what you get. You may be able to offer your client higher audio quality!

Now let's take a look at another example.

Example 2: Mood Music DVD

The client has requested a mood music DVD with lots of different audio formats:

- (6) 25-minute video tracks—mostly lock shots on a tripod of waves, rain, dockside, birds, and a waterfall. Bird footage has lots of motion of flying birds.

- (1) AC-3—surround 5.1 channel mix @ .768 Mbps

- (1) PCM—stereo @ 1.5 Mbps

- (1) DTS—5-channel @ 1.5 Mbps

- (1) Menu—no video with (1) overlay

- No subtitles

The client has requested a DVD-5 delivery because their duplicator is outfitted for this type of disc reproduction only.

Again, let's run the numbers and see what we come up with.

Bit Budget Formula #1:

MAX Video Only Encode Bit Rate = 9.8 Mbps–(Audio Streams + Subpictures)

MAX Video Only Encode Bit Rate = 9.8 Mbps–[(.768 Mbps (AC3) + 1.5 Mbps (PCM) +1.5 Mbps (DTS)]

MAX Video Only Encode Bit Rate = 9.8 Mbps–3.768 Mbps

MAX Video Only Encode Bit Rate = 6.032 Mbps

Bit Budget Formula #2:

Average Encoding Rate =

Disc Type Total Mbits divided by [(# of min. of video) x 60 sec.]

Average Encoding Rate = [36,096 Mbits (DVD-5) divided by [(150 minutes (video) x 60]

Average Encoding Rate = 36,096 divided by 9,000

Average Encoding Rate = 4.01 Mbps

Bit Budget Formula #3:

Video Only Target Bit Rate =

(Average Encoding Rate)–(Audio Streams + Subpictures)

Video Only Target Bit Rate = 4.01 Mbps—[(.768 Mbps (AC3) +1.5 Mbps (PCM) +1.5 Mbps (DTS)]

Video Only Target Bit Rate = 4.01 Mbps –3.768 Mbps

Video Only Target Bit Rate = .842 Mbps

Example 2 Discussion:

So what does it all mean? Let's take a look at what we've got.

Here is what we calculated:

1. *MAX Video Encode Bit Rate = 6.032 Mbps*

2. *AVG. Video Encode Rate = 4.01 Mbps*

3. *Video Only Target Bit Rate = .842 Mbps*

Basically, these numbers should trip some red flags. Our video target bit rate is below 1 Mbps. It will be difficult to achieve decent-looking video with MPEG-2, even though our footage is mostly lock-shot tripod with not a ton of motion. The 6.032 Mbps may seem like enough headroom, but if that bird footage needs to be encoded at a higher rate because of the motion, it will skew the average throughput and will most likely fill the pipe. Also, any higher bit rates for longer sections of the video will most likely fill up the disc beyond the capacity of the DVD-5. In this case, I would recommend to the client that they consider the following: Instead of the PCM stereo mix, they might try a Dolby stereo encode at about .192 Mbps. This will save them about 1.3 Mbps. If they insisted on the PCM format because the audio quality is more important than the visuals, you might suggest using a DVD-9 format, which will give them plenty of room for all assets at a much higher bit rate. If they insist on all formats and video on the DVD-5, then I would make them some encoded video samples ahead of time at the target bit rate of .842 Mbps and get them to sign off on the video quality before you deliver the final mastered disc.

The main point is that by bit budgeting ahead of time, we can see these potential problems *before* we spend valuable time encoding, and come up with the different alternatives for the client.

Conclusion

As the technology moves forward, there are current specifications on the table for new, higher-density discs than are commercially available today. The blue laser ("Blu-ray") and HD-DVD specifications will be in the mainstream in the near future. These discs will hold upwards of 23 GB of data. So by doing the math from

Table 6.1, we find out that with the 4% headroom there are 176,640 Mbits of space on these new discs. You might think that's a ton more space and bit budgeting will become obsolete, but you will still need to plan your projects with the bit budgeting formulas, because the video and audio content streams for high-definition material will easily fill these larger discs as well.

While bit budgeting may seem like a boring and time-consuming process, it is an essential part of successful DVD production. Without proper planning, you will attempt to author your projects and you will find the throughput "pipe" filled at certain points, or that your disc simply does not have the room to fit all of the media you are attempting to put on it at a quality level your client is expecting. At the end of the day you will miss your deadlines due to time-consuming re-encoding and have to deal with those irate customers. The bit budget is also a great way to manage your client's expectations on asset quality. Should you find that there are just too many assets for the delivery format your client has requested, you will know sooner than later and can start those client discussions before it becomes a nightmare production. It's all about proper planning.

CHAPTER 7

Printing Your Final Mixes

Once you've completed your surround mix in Pro Tools, you have to prepare it for delivery. There are several different ways to output a multichannel project, and sometimes the method you use will depend on the requirements of the client. It's very important at this point to pay attention to your channel configurations, making sure you deliver a master with the correct multichannel assignments.

Creating a Multichannel Bounce

1. Select the length audio program you would like to include in the bounce.

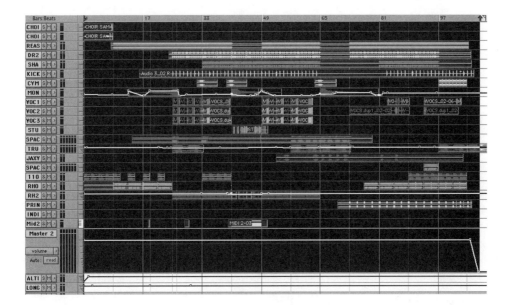

Fig. 7-1: Audio selection

2. Select File > Bounce to Disk

3. A Bounce Options screen will appear. Make sure your Bounce Source is the I/O output for your surround mix. Select Multiple Mono to create six discrete mono channels for a 5.1 mix. I like to use Best Conversion Quality, and Convert After Bounce.

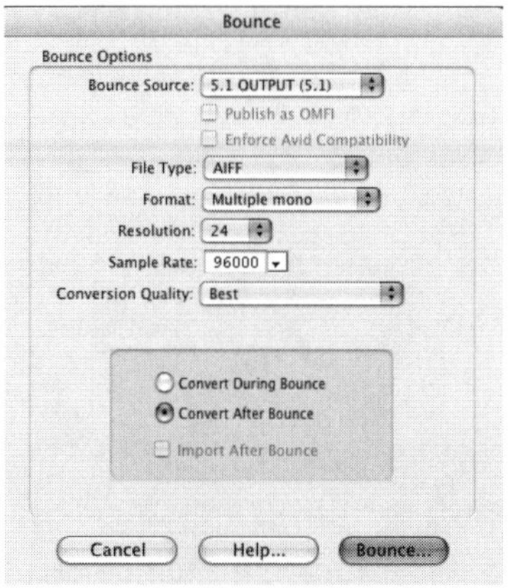

Fig. 7-2: Bounce Options window

4. Select > Bounce. A Save Bounce As screen will appear, prompting you to select a drive. I like to create a new folder, named after the project, then create a sub-folder with the name of the specific bounce, and a date. For example: "5.1 Good Tune Bounce, 7.4.04."

5. The bounced files will then appear as they do below. Each will be auto-labeled in Pro Tools with the prefix "5.1 Good Tune Bounce 7.4.04 C (Center), 5.1 Good Tune Bounce 7.4.04 L (Left), etc.—including Lf (LFE), Ls (Left Surround), R (Right Front), and Rs (Right Surround).

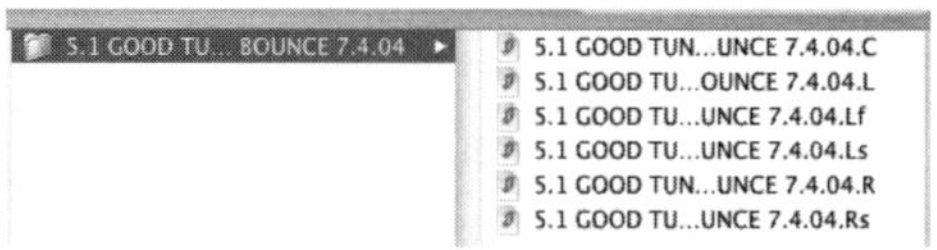

Fig. 7-3: Six channels of bounced audio

Printing to Tape or Hard Disk

In addition to leaving your printed bounces in Pro Tools, multichannel mixes and/or stems can also be printed to a variety of tape and hard-disk recorders. Always try to print your mixes using digital I/O, so you avoid any kind of unnecessary analog conversion.

Many multichannel mixes with resolutions of up to 16-bit/48kHz are delivered in Tascam DA-88 format. For higher-resolution audio (up to 24-bit), Tascam DA-98 or DA-78 MDM formats are often used. All of the above machines can accept timecode printing as well. Often when outputting a project to such machines, you may have to patch your hardware accordingly, as the channel configuration required on the tape may not match what is coming out of Pro Tools.

Other common print formats include Tascam MMR-8 or Genex hard-disk recorders, as well as good old analog tape. Even those old 20-bit ADAT machines make excellent delivery platforms for 16- to 20-bit mixes—and they provide an additional way to back up your multichannel mixes.

You can actually use whatever recorder you prefer, as long as it meets the requirements of:

- Track count

- Bit resolution

- Sample rate

- Digital I/O (always preferred)

- Timecode synchronization if needed

- 9-pin control if needed

- Word clock I/O if needed

- Robust format for repeated playback

Layback to VTR

Layback to video is sometimes required for projects (see story below). Certain video decks, such as the Panasonic D5 HD/SD VTR, can accept up to eight channels of audio. This allows you to print not only a six-channel surround mix, but a two-channel stereo or Lt/Rt mix as well. More commonly, however, multichannel mixes are delivered either as Pro Tools files or on an MDR or hard-disk recorder.

Additional Elements to Provide

When printing, it's important to include at least 30 seconds of tone (preferably 1kHz at –20dBFS). Make sure to include documentation as to what tracks are printed on what channels. *This is very important!* Too many times I've gotten projects in that did not have the channels documented, and I literally had to spend time plugging in various configurations to confirm the proper layout. Check with the chart below if you're unsure how to print your mixes.

Channel Assignments

ITU and SMPTE Standard

- CH1: Left Front
- CH2: Right Front
- CH3: Center
- CH4: LFE
- CH5: Left Surround
- CH6: Right Surround

DTS Standard

- CH1: Left Front
- CH2: Right Front
- CH3: Left Surround
- CH4: Right Surround
- CH5: Center
- CH6: LFE

Film Standard

- CH1: Left Front
- CH2: Right Front
- CH3: Left Surround
- CH4: Right Surround
- CH5: Center
- CH6: LFE

NOTE: CH7 and CH8 are often used for an separate stereo mix regardless of format, or for Lt/Rt (Left total/Right total) prints.

Also note what filter frequency was used for the LFE and/or bass-management reference, and at what reference level (in SPL) you mixed and calibrated your system. Include additional important information such as timecode, frame rates, and bit and sample resolution.

Interview With Dave Glaser

Below is an interview with Dave Glaser, multichannel engineer/sound-designer at Gizmo Studios in New York City. In it, we discuss a good real-world example of how surround sound is delivered to a client. As Dave points out, it's not always your choice, as a mixer, as to what elements get placed in a surround mix. Sometimes it's the call of the production company and/or producer of a spot.

Q: What was this particular surround mix for, and what were the delivery requirements?

A: This was an HD (high-definition) presentation for TNT and Regal Cinemas. It was promoting the making of TNT's original movie on Evel Knievel. The primary direction was that they wanted an absence of crowd sounds, because they said when it plays in the theater, those sounds might get lost in what's real and what's not. The other thing they wanted was a shadow of the front Left/Right mix in the surrounds, because they felt it would increase the size of the audio sweet spot in the theater. That also goes for the narrations and bites and interviews as well. The crossover had to be set to 100Hz or lower. They also wanted the surround channels boosted an additional 4–8dB, as their theaters are large and they wanted "full cinematic presentation."

Q: So how did you handle the Lt/Rt mix?

A: The elements were mixed in Dolby Surround Tools. We first created a discrete 5.1 mix with all the elements, as you might expect. Then we made an Lt/Rt from that mix. Basically, that Lt/Rt is a fail-safe for theaters that don't have a 5.1 setup. It's really just a Pro Logic Mix.

Q: How did you specifically handle the Dolby encode/decode process in Pro Tools?

A: I took the finished 5.1 mix and created a new session with a Quad Aux track with an LCRS setup in the I/O page. Then I instantiated the Dolby Surround Encoder plug-in, which automatically turns the Quad Aux track into a stereo Aux track. My mix went in there, and I monitored that by creating a stereo Aux bus and putting on the Dolby Surround decoder plug-in. That turns it into a Quad output for L, C, R, and mono Surround, routed directly out of Pro Tools into the monitors. You do have to juggle a few patches to ensure your Left is left and Right is right, but it's just for checking.

Dolby suggests first making a four-track LCRS input by taking the LCRS bus and assigning it to the input of that channel. On the insert, you put the Dolby Surround Encoder plug-in. Now it will take the four channels—Left, Center, Right, and mono surrounds—and turn them into two channels of Lt/Rt. Then I created a stereo Aux bus and assigned a decoder to it. The Dolby decoder will turn it into a four-channel LCRS decode, which routes out of Pro Tools. Finally, you check it in LCRS, stereo, and mono for compatibility.

Q: What about the sub?

A: Actually, you send your low-frequency signals to the Center channel, since there is no discrete LFE in Dolby Surround. What happens is that anything below 100Hz goes into the sub. It's a bit odd, but it works.

Q: How did you deliver it to the client?

A: We went straight to the Panasonic D-5 high-definition video deck. On channels 7 and 8 were the Lt/Rt delivery, and the discrete surround mix was printed on channels 1 through 6.

Mastering Surround Sound

8

Why Master Your Surround Tracks with a Mastering Engineer?

Mastering in surround sound is a mystery to some and an essential part of the record-making process to others. Mastering, not only for surround, is actually many things:

- It helps create a uniform, continuous sound for the project. This is especially important in this day and age when multiple mixers, engineers, and producers are often involved in delivering a final product.

- It can add that "sheen" that is quite hard to achieve (and define, until you hear it) without the proper mastering gear.

- A good mastering engineer can take a good mix and make it great. They can make a great mix amazing, but rarely can they make a bad mix good.

- It can make your mixes louder, but be careful with this. Experienced mastering engineers often resist the artist/producer's insistence to make everything loud, because doing so reduces dynamic range. Experience usually dictates what's best.

- Mastering, through any combination of the effective use of EQ, compression, leveling, and careful listening, is usually worth the financial investment!

Surround mastering can truly take your sound to the next level. Apart from knowing that a professional-sounding product will be achieved by using a good multichannel mastering engineer, it's invaluable to have another person listen to your mix objectively. They may hear things you don't, because you were either too fatigued or too involved to make accurate sonic decisions. When working with five or more channels, this objective scrutiny becomes even more important.

Also, in most cases, the mastering engineer has made a substantial investment in equipment, allowing them to hear what you may not have heard in your room. Since surround mixing usually involves LFE information, a properly "tuned" room can help define the low end of your mix. You don't want to hand the consumer a product that overwhelms their subwoofer, or, on the other hand, doesn't deliver enough low end. It's good to know that a mastering engineer can take care of most, if not all, of the low-end issues that may be present in your mix.

I can say without question that the end results delivered to me by a professional multichannel mastering engineer made my mixes sound better. If you're not sure that the final bounces will get mastered at a facility or not, I suggest *not* adding additional processing on the final bounce—such as compression, limiting, or EQ— unless there is a specific sonic treatment you want to achieve. That's one of the things you're paying the mastering engineer to do, and probably one of the things they do best. You certainly can, however, make two final masters—one with processing and one without.

Don't forget, when your mastered mixes sound better to the public, your reputation tends to become stronger. When your reputation becomes stronger, you often get more work. It's simply a reality of the business!

Interview With Airshow Mastering's David Glasser

Airshow Mastering, in sunny Boulder, Colorado, is one of the premier facilities in the field of stereo and multichannel mastering. The 20-year old award-winning company, which also operates out of Springfield, Virginia, has always prided itself on utilizing the latest techniques and technologies while maintaining its roots in the past.

Airshow's founder and Chief Engineer is David Glasser, who has received multiple Grammy Awards, including a 2003 Grammy Award for the *Screamin' and Hollerin' the Blues: The World of Charley Patton* project. Since Glasser and Airshow receive a sizable portion of their incoming work as projects mixed in Pro Tools, I thought he could provide readers some insight on the subject of surround mastering.

Q: What Pro Tools formats come into Airshow?

A: It's an even mix of SDIIs, WAVs, and AIFFs. Actually, on our end, it doesn't matter what file type you send us; we'll work with them all. Source audio comes in on CD-R, DVD-R, and increasingly, FireWire hard drives.

Q: How about high-resolution files?

A: We get quite a bit of 96k stuff. You almost have to go out of your way not to do hi-res these days.

Fig. 8-1: David Glasser

Q: What formats have you delivered out of Airshow that came in as Pro Tools files and/or mixes?

A: We've mastered CDs, audio for DVD-Video, DVD-Audio, and SA-CD titles.

Q: Are the surround mixes always six-channel 5.1 deliveries?

A: Usually it's five- or six-channel mixes, as sometime people don't print an LFE channel. We had one producer bring in a Pro Tools session for surround that had additional stem mixes, which worked out great. We were able to tweak the channels further—especially the surround channels—since it was a live concert mix. As we were going along, we were able to not only make level changes, but also wrap the mix around the listener and better integrate the rear channels into the soundfield.

Q: What is the first step you take when receiving a mix for a DVD-V or DVD-A project?

A: For my work I use Sonic HD, so I'll open those files up directly in my system, whether it's for DVD-A or DVD-V. I tend to use the same kind of processing as I would do for a CD: analog, PCM, or a combination. If it's for SA-CD, I generally try to avoid additional PCM processing and use either analog or the DSD processing in the Sony Sonoma.

Q: What do you feel is a common mistake you've found with the LFE channel?

A: Lots of people don't even use it, which is often a good idea. Unless you have some interesting effects, you really don't always need it. Bass management will usually make sure there's something pumping in your sub. Some common problems would be just level issues, but occasionally you'll see where people have put the same information in the LFE that's already in the mains. That will, of course, cause problems when you kick in the bass management, as you'll then get double the information.

Q: Do you have to filter frequencies off the five main channels at all?

A: No, I usually leave them full range. I might bleed in a little bit into the LFE channel, if they want to have that information there. If you filter the main channels, then you are really cheating the people who do have full-range playback on their mains.

Q: Do you check bass management?

A: Oh yes, we always check the bass-managed signal through a Martinsound ManagerMax bass manager that I patch in. It allows me to switch between the audio signal going through the full-range main speakers and then the bass manager, which rolls off the mains and directs it to the subwoofer. This makes sure that in a consumer system there won't be any weird problems in the low end.

Q: When you receive a surround mix for DVD-V, do you watch the video playback?

A: Yes, we do. We watch video with a beta SP machine and lock it to the playback of the session. We usually watch the video first as we're listening, then figure out what kind of mastering changes need to be done; then we'll work without picture. Then we will watch the video again with the final print, to make sure it all works.

Q: How do you typically deliver a session back to a client?

A: For refs we can do DTS CDs, or I'll deliver WAV files that they can port back into their Pro Tools system and hear it like that. We'll also soon be delivering DVD-V references with Dolby AC-3, PCM, and DTS audio on them.

Mastering With Pro Tools

Another reality of the "business" of surround sound is that not all projects have the budget to be mastered at a mastering facility. For those of you who choose to master your end result inside Pro Tools, there's quite a powerful arsenal of tools to do so. See Chapter 9 for a listing of surround plug-ins and how they can help your final mix.

It's common in the final phase of surround mastering to add some level changes, as well as EQ and compression. Obviously, every mix will have its own individual needs. Once your project sounds the way you want it to, you can either insert a multichannel or multi-mono plug-in to process your mix. The approach should be the same as stereo, but pay careful attention to channel balances and the LFE/Sub information. Mastering surround on your own should be done with caution. I can't stress enough how important it is to check your mix on as many systems as possible before releasing it to the public. If something doesn't sound correct, it will give you time to go back and get it right.

The most important thing is to try to ensure that the consumer hears a balanced mix. If you have taken the time to properly calibrate your room and monitoring setup, as well as carefully mix your tracks, the results should translate properly. This is one of the hardest aspects of surround-sound mixing—trying to know what the consumer will hear. The variables are almost endless; five or more speakers, good and bad rooms, surround speakers that may be too high or low, too far or too close to the listener, etc. All you can do is deliver a product that sounds right to *you*.

Now go out and create a surround mix!

CHAPTER 9

Software Plug-Ins for Surround Sound

Pro Tools provides an ever-expanding array of optional plug-ins for surround production, both from third-party developers and from Digidesign themselves. These can range from multichannel reverbs, metering, equalization, and limiting, to tools for tuning your room and encoding audio. Plug-ins can be multi-mono, mono, stereo, or multichannel formats.

As with traditional mono or stereo plug-ins, they can be invaluable when producing surround content. In this chapter, we'll take a look at some of them.

Surround Plug-Ins

Waves 360

www.waves.com

For those who want to do surround sound mixing with Pro Tools, I can't recommend this bundle enough. Designed to work on the Mac platform for Pro Tools HD, Accel, and Mix Systems, the Waves 360 Surround Toolkit is a collection of seven separate software elements used in multichannel production: surround reverb, limiter, manager, imager, panner, compressor, and mixdown plug-in, plus a few extras.

The M360 is a very important element of this bundle. This is the surround-managing part of the Toolkit, providing bass-management and studio-monitoring calibration based upon the ITU standard. It features two plug-in components: the Manager and Mixdown. The Manager is inserted last on a master surround output and handles monitor calibration and setup. It also allows for software adjustments of speaker angles to work with the panner, as well as per-channel gain and delay for level and phase alignments. Mixdown can be inserted directly after the Manager, allowing for preview of mono, stereo, LCR (Left/Center/Right), and LCRS (surround) imaging.

Fig. 9-1: Waves M360

This duo is vital to surround mixing engineers and has really helped ensure that my surround mixes translate well to the public. The bass-management tools provided by the M360 allow your professional surround monitors to respond like a typical consumer home system. I also use it to calibrate my monitors for proper playback.

The S360 is a surround panner and imaging tool. The panner allows you to set separate width and rotation for mono, stereo, five-channel, or 5.1-channel sources. The imager is an enhanced panner, with shuffling for additional low-frequency width, as well as room model early reflections. Simply put, the imager makes your source sound like it's in a controllable room.

Fig. 9-2: Waves S360

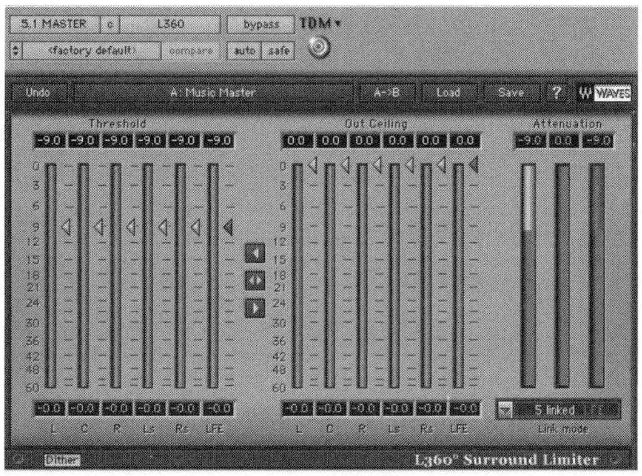

Fig. 9-3: Waves L360

I often automate the imager distances to create really cool effects. You can actually hot-swap between the panner and the imager, and all the common controls will retain their existing settings. Panning in surround is essential, and these two tools offer many options.

The L360 is a surround peak limiter and level maximizer based upon the popular L1 and L2 UltraMaximizers. With resolution up to 96kHz, it has Waves' ARC Auto Release Control and brickwall peak limiting. It offers five different link modes and three separate sidechains.

In the current world of surround mixing, not every title gets mastered properly. I often insert the L360 on the end of my surround master fader to give it that extra kick that allows the mix to punch through the speakers. I'm a big fan of how the L2 sounds on my mixes, and this is just as good. Note that I do not print with it when I'm taking my work to a mastering house; this is one of the processes you would best let an experienced mastering engineer handle.

The C360 is a surround soft-knee compressor that also works on five or 5.1 channels with flexible link modes. It features similar functionality and control as

Fig. 9-4: Waves C360

the L360, also featuring ARC, but with a different sonic characteristic. It can be inserted on any 5.0 or 5.1 track, Aux input, or master fader and actually attenuates the signal before the threshold level is reached, with increased attenuation after the threshold is passed.

I use the C360 in a similar fashion as the L360, but mostly when I need a bit more "squash" on the program material. It works especially well on heavy rock mixes that need to be compressed.

Fig. 9-5: Waves R360

The R360 is an excellent-sounding 5.1/5.0 reverb that creates only tails and not early reflections (early reflections are generated in the S360 surround imager mentioned above). The R360 also includes controls for the reverb sound and mix properties, specifically designed for multichannel production.

I use the R360 on drums, guitars, and vocals. It's especially strong on strings, where the smoothness really adds depth without harshness. It provides a powerful and effective sense of envelopment.

Finally, there's the LFE 360 Low Pass Filter and IDR 360 Bit Requantizer. The LFE 360 is a 7th-order filter that lets you preview how an encoder's LFE filter will

Fig. 9-6: Waves LFE 360

PRO TOOLS SURROUND SOUND MIXING

Fig. 9-7: Waves IDR 360

affect your mixes. Recommended placement is just before the M360 manager. IDR 360 allows for multichannel word-length reduction with flexible dither and noise shaping capabilities.

The LFE 360 ensures proper low-end monitoring, and I've used the IDR 360 to send hi-res surround mixes to those who can't play back hi-res audio.

Audio Ease Altiverb

www.audioease.com

The existence of plug-in–based Impulse Response (IR) reverbs have only come about in recent years, due to the massive increases in computing power. Impulse Responses are not models of rooms, halls, churches, or digital gear. They are actual samples of each, reproduced using a technology called *convolution*—hence the term "convolution engine." Simply put, either a spike of sound (a cap gun, for example), or a full sweep tone is sent into the space you want to capture. Using a microphone array, the IR of the space is recorded. By using a convolution engine combined with an Impulse Response, you have "real" reverb at your fingertips.

The mathematical calculations involved in creating good convolution-based Impulse Responses are massive. Altiverb was the first IR plug-in on the market, and has been out for a few years now. They recently released a new Version 4, offering tone control, parameter automation, and more important, better performance to lighten the CPU load.

Fig. 9-8: Audio Ease Altiverb

Altiverb also has a massive Impulse Response library, posted not only by the company, but also by a legion of devoted users. I've gotten some beautiful IRs from their website: www.audioease.com/IR, which even provides a search function. You can type in "studios," for example, and a listing of the currently available Studio IRs pops up. How do Cello, Westlake, and several Bill Putnam rooms sound? Actually, as I sit here, I just downloaded one I didn't have yet: the Wiener Konzerthaus in Austria. Within just a few minute's time, I now have mono-to-stereo and stereo-to-stereo Impulse Responses, as well as mono-to-quad and stereo-to-quad IRs. Think about what we have at our disposal—the ability to go online and download a world-class acoustic space and then use it immediately! Also, with Altiverb, you can sample your own acoustic spaces, or even some of your outboard gear. I downloaded a nice EMT 250 Plate IR that I use all the time on vocals. Altiverb runs on G4 and G5 Macs and works with MAS, HTDM, RTAS, VST, and Audio Units.

Waves IR-1

www.waves.com

The IR-1 Impulse Response reverb comes with a number of pre-loaded factory presets, but it also comes with two CDs full of IRs. CD#1 is called Sampled Acoustics and features first-class opera houses, concert halls, cathedrals, studios, and other spaces. CD#2 is called Virtual Acoustics and contains sampled IRs from synthetically generated and pre-processed spaces, as well as a nice set of classic reference reverb hardware sounds. The Waves team traveled to Italy, Japan, Israel, Australia, and the U.S. to gather these IRs, using a custom recording setup/method developed in conjunction with Professor Angelo Farina of the University of Parma.

Fig. 9-9: Waves IR-1

PRO TOOLS SURROUND SOUND MIXING

As you would expect from Waves, this plug-in is quite easy to use. The GUI can be quickly navigated without reading the manual. The included PDF is full of information, and you can go to their website (www.waves.com) to get as deep into it as you want. To get started, you simply load an IR from the Load menu, which breaks out a submenu of choices for all IRs in your folder. For most presets, Waves has included two choices per IR: Impulse Response and Reset or just Impulse Response. IR/Reset fully resets all the plug-in parameters to flat, except for the Wet/Dry Slider and the Direct On/Off switch.

Now to the heart of what makes this plug-in special. Beyond all the great-sounding IRs—my favorite of which happens to be Trinity Church in New York (where I've recorded often due to its amazing acoustics)—you can tweak the heck out of this thing! First, you see the IR on a scrollable graph, showing level in dB vertically and time horizontally. You can change the sample's reverb time using Ratio, RT60, and Convolution Length, up to six seconds. You can also alter the Size as a ratio of the original IR, and change the Density, Resonance, and Decorrelation control, making stereo out of a mono IR.

There is also a Dry/Wet control, and the IR-1 separates the "Direct," "Early Reflections," and "Reverb Tail" portions of the impulse response. Each element has its own gain and predelay value. There is also control over CPU mode, with Full or Low (which slightly compromises the resolution, saving upwards of 45% CPU cycle, with an average savings of about 20%). A Reverb Envelope lets you graphically change the nature of the IR, for such effects as gating, flanging, and fast or slow decays. There is another graph for Reverb Damping and my favorite—the Reverb EQ, which is a 4-band paragraphic EQ. When any of these overall changes is made, the IR-1 automatically mutes the audio and recalculates the math—a very brief process on my dual $2GH_3$ G5 Mac.

Waves designed the IR-1 to intelligently use the host computer's processing power, since Impulse Response reverbs notoriously require a lot of math! As for latency, Waves notes that the IR-1 has none inherently since the Dry path goes directly to the output, but there is an 11.6 ms processing latency at 44.1/48kHz and 5.3 ms at 88.2/96kHz.

Trillium Lane Labs TL Space

www.tllabs.com

Trillium Lane Labs TL Space is a highly useable TDM convolution reverb that features support for TDM, HTDM, RTAS, and AudioSuite for Pro Tools|HD and HD Accel systems. There is also a Native edition supporting RTAS and AudioSuite for Pro Tools|HD or Pro Tools LE systems running 6.2 or newer software. Besides being mono through 5.0 multichannel capable, it provides a collection of Impulse Response folders including halls, churches, rooms, chambers, plates, springs, digital reverbs, post production, Tiny Spaces, and effects.

Fig. 9-10: Trillium Lane TL Space

The "plasma"-like faders allow for easy control over input and output levels, early and late reflections, and wet, dry, and decay time. There are buttons for Levels, Delays, Early, Reverb, Decay, and Reset functionality. The GUI features a screenshot of the Impulse Response, which can also be viewed as a waveform. Next to that sits the Input and Output meters, which assign themselves according to the channel selection chosen (5.0 provides Left, Right, Center, Left Surround, and Right Surround outs).

Digidesign ReVibe

www.digidesign.com

ReVibe is a new TDM plug-in designed exclusively for the HD Accel card. This reverb modeling tool includes nine new reverb algorithms and over 200 room types and early reflections, all running up to 96kHz, natively. The reverb algorithms can process audio at 96kHz without sample-rate conversion.

ReVibe runs in mono, stereo, and surround, and is built upon the user interface of Digidesign's Reverb One plug-in. It features a flexible set of room modeling controls allowing the user to adjust room colorations, early reflections, ambience, density, and presence. It was engineered to utilize the power increase provided by the 321 DSP chips on the Accel card, so it won't run on previous-generation TDM systems.

The layout is quite similar to Reverb One, with a few additional parameters. In the Levels section, there is of course the input level, but there are also sliders to control the front, center, rear reverb, and rear ER (early reflections). There is also the ability to turn off those ERs, via a master ER on/off or just a rear ER on/off.

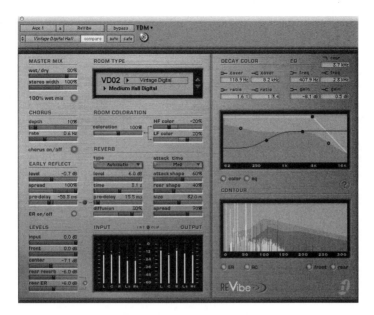

Fig. 9-11: Digidesign Revibe

In the Reverb section, there is a Rear Shape slider along with the more traditional Level, Time, Pre-delay, Diffusion, Attack Shape, Size, and spread. There's also a pull-down menu to choose the reverb type, with various choices ranging from natural to small. Attack time also has a pull-down menu, with choices of short, medium or long.

The Metering section features input and output of L, C, R, Ls, and Rs signal. It's interesting to watch the surround meters react when feeding a stereo signal into ReVibe—you see the L and R meters react on input, along with the corresponding L, C, R, Ls, and Rs meters reacting to how you've tweaked your reverb.

Also slightly different from Reverb One is the Decay Color section, with low and high frequency crossovers and low and high frequency ratios. EQ parameters include low and high frequency shelving, low and high Gain (high boosts both mid and high), and a high-frequency Rear Cut, which rolls off high frequencies in the early reflections and reverb tail in the rear channels only, a parameter which is applied in addition to any global EQ. There's also a Room Coloration section with a coloration slider and HF and LF color sliders.

As with Reverb One, there are EQ and Contour (called Color in R-one) windows, allowing for easy grasping of EQ points and display of early reflections and reverb contour, as well as the front- and rear-channel contours and reflections.

In the Room Type graphic window, users can choose an overall menu of Vintage Digital, Springs, Plates, Churches, etc. You can also use the traditional method of selecting presets from the plug-ins menu selector. There the listings are more direct in nature, such as EMT 250 Hall, Long Inverse Room, Airport Terminal, Bathroom, and Orchestral Ambience, among many others. In the plug-in pull-down menu, the

ReVibe choices are stereo, stereo/LCR, stereo/LCRS, stereo/Quad, stereo/5.0, and stereo 5.1. The letters for each selection turn white at the bottom of the Input and Output meters to reflect your choice. This plug-in sounds amazing in surround!

Sony Oxford Dynamics

www.sonyplugins.com

The Sony Oxford Dynamics plug-in is a six-channel bus compressor for surround applications. It is highly flexible, offering separate Gate, Expander, Compressor, Limiter, Side Chain EQ, and Warmth functionality. All parameters are fully automatable, and the signal path insertion noise and distortion are incredibly low—below –130dB.

The plug-in works just like Sony's Oxford OXF-R3 console—you have to "arm" each separate section by clicking the In button. Once you've done that, if you press the Access button, the GUI will display the parameter selections of that selection. In other words, if you arm and select Gate, you can then adjust the various parameters on the plug-in interface. This works for each section, allowing a massive amount of control in a small quantity of space.

Other features include input and output metering, as well as gain-reduction meters for Gate, Exp (Expander), Comp, and Limit. There's also a large Gain Transfer display on the lower-right side of the plug-in, showing your parameter adjustments in real-time. It's quite useful to have all this information in front of you in one single display, and it makes the whole tweaking process quite simple.

There are some hidden gems within the Dynamics plug-in, including a Time constant and type selector, offering selection of the compressor's time-constant dependency laws: Normal, Linear, and Classic (like a dbx 160). Believe me, you

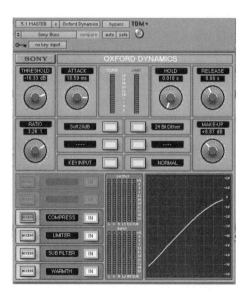

Fig. 9-12: Sony Oxford Dynamics in 5.1 Mode

PRO TOOLS SURROUND SOUND MIXING

can hear the difference when switching between them, as some are more aggressive than others. Indeed, they all have their "sound" and I happen to prefer Linear.

There is also a Soft Ratio selector, which selects the soft ratio in 5dB steps, up to –20dB below threshold. The Warmth function adds a smooth overdrive to the overall sound—subtle but useful. The compressor also has a Makeup Gain control of +24dB.

Digidesign Impact

www.digidesign.com

Impact is a console-style mix bus TDM compressor for the Pro Tools Accel system. It can handle surround mixes of up to 7.1 channels, with sample rates up to 192kHz. This plug-in is extremely easy to use, with four selectable compression ratios and variable controls available for Attack, Threshold, Release, and Make-up Gain. Other features include digital I/O metering and a cool analog-style Gain Reduction meter. It can be used across a master fader, or on individual channels.

Fig. 9-13: Digidesign Impact in 6.1 (in stereo mode)

Software for Encoding Surround

As will be discussed in Chapter 10, your finished multichannel mixes must be encoded for surround playback. Of course, you can use hardware encoders for Dolby, DTS, or SRS Circle Surround. However, software is also available to let you handle these tasks simply and efficiently, right on your desktop.

SRS Labs Circle Surround

www.srslabs.com

SRS Circle Surround TDM Pro is a surround encode/decode plug-in suite that offers delivery of up to 6.1 channels (L, C, R, Ls, Cs, Rs, LFE) over any stereo media or transmission. It also offers real-time monitoring through the entire encode/decode process and is compatible with such codecs as MP3, AC-3, AAC, and Windows Media.

There is full support for Pro Tools surround control and panning, along with control surface support for Pro Control, HUI, etc. It's identical in performance to the company's SRS CSD-07 Circle Surround Hardware (encode and decode) and it supports sample rates up to 96kHz. System requirements are Pro Tools HD 6.0 TDM or higher, running either Mac OSX or Windows XP. This plug-in is great for Pro Tools users because you can take an encoded Lt/Rt mix and burn it onto a CD. A consumer without a surround decoder in their playback system will hear the standard stereo mix (or mono). However, a consumer with a surround decoder (6.1 playback requires Circle Surround II decoding) will hear a surround mix. Very cool indeed.

You can send the two-channel output from the Circle Surround encoder to MPEG, AC3, AAC, DAB, IBOC, WMA, RA, SD or HD Broadcasting, or PCM. In fact, the market is starting to see a handful of DVDs using Circle Surround as the default stereo/PCM track, as well offering a discrete mix like DTS.

SRS Circle Surround Encoder plug-in features include:

- Up to 6.1-channel input delivering a two-channel output

- 44.1, 48, 96kHz sample-rate support

- Lowpass filter on the LFE channel

- Will accept stems in LCR, LCRS, 5.1, 5,1, 6.0, 6.1 formats

- Selectable highpass filter on the L,C,R, Ls, Cs, Rs channels

- Supports bit rates as low as 64 kbps and above 192 kbps

Fig. 9-14: SRS Labs Circle Surround

SRS Circle Surround Decoder plug-in features include:

- Up to 6.1-channel output from two-channel input

- Same sample-rate support as encoder (up to 96kHz)

- Decode modes for Circle Surround, stereo, mono, LCRS

- Individual channel output trim controls

- SRS TruBass and SRS Dialog Clarity post-processing

A Circle Surround encoded file can be decoded by the following:

1. Circle Surround or Circle Surround II

2. Logic 7

3. DTS NEO: 6

4. Dolby Pro Logic II

5. Dolby Pro Logic or Dolby Surround

Dolby Surround Tools 3.0

www.dolby.com

Dolby Surround Tools lets TDM users produce Dolby Surround (discussed in Chapter 10) by providing both and encoder and decoder plug-ins. The software's surround encode process matches Dolby's SEU4 and DP563 hardware encoders. Dolby Surround Tools supports sample rates up to 96kHz.

Fig. 9-15: Dolby Surround Tools

Apple A.Pack

A.Pack is software for encoding Dolby Digital AC-3 files. This is not a TDM plug-in, as it is part of Apple's DVD Studio Pro 3 software package. However, it's extremely easy to use, as long as your source files are 48kHz and all of the same length. By simply dragging and dropping the files into the A.Pack window and making a few menu selections, A.Pack will encode and output a single AC-3 file for you.

There are many options in the Audio Coding Mode dropdown menu. With the Enable Low Frequency Effects box selected, A.Pack will output a .1 or LFE channel as well. You can also select your chosen data rate and Dialog Normalization level (setting it to −31dBFS will not alter any levels at all).

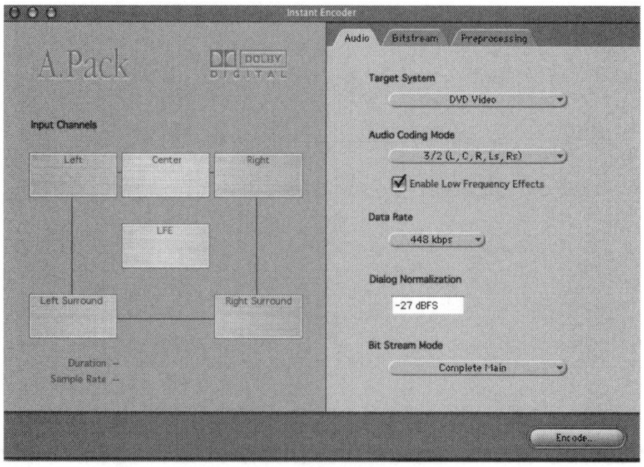

Fig. 9-16: Apple A.Pack

As you might expect, you can select various Downmix settings to provide a proper stereo or mono mix for those without surround playback capabilities. There is also an AC-3 Monitor included in the overall bundle, allowing you to monitor and decode an AC-3 stream. Note that DVD Studio Pro 3 will let you import DTS files into your project, but it does not provide an encoder.

Vegas 5+DVD

Sony Media Software's Vegas+DVD Production Suite (for PC only) includes 5.1-channel AC-3 encoding. It features variable data rates up to 640 kbps, with sample rates up to 48kHz. There are various bitstream, downmix, LFE, and Mix level options included. Users can also encode for the WMA-9 Windows Media format for surround streaming over the web, etc. There is a free trial version available at www.sony.com/mediasoftware.

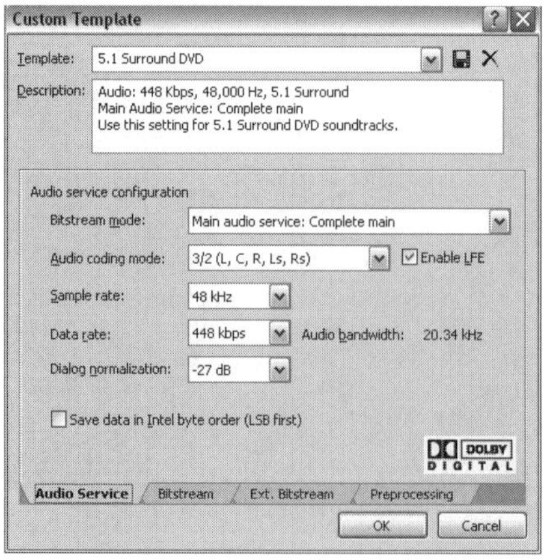

Fig. 9-17: Sony Media Vegas DVD

PRO TOOLS SURROUND SOUND MIXING

External Surround Processing Hardware

Apart from software-based plug-ins, surround sound producers have the option of using hardware processors. Interfacing with Pro Tools is usually accomplished via digital I/O, but if the interface boxes have analog cards, they can also be used. Let's take a brief look at some of the major devices on the market and what they do.

Eventide H8000

www.eventide.com

Eventide's H8000 Ultra-Harmonizer is a processor with over a thousand preset algorithms. It features eight channels of AES/EBU, ADAT, and stereo S/PDIF digital I/O at full 24-bit resolution, an easy-to-use search engine for presets, "Anything-to-Anything" routing capability, and support for a PC graphic editor/development tool.

There are over 80 5.1 presets, as well as full 5.1 reverb algorithms and effects that operate up to 96kHz. Like the company's popular Orville model (but with more powerful DSP functionality), it also features choruses, FM panners, vocoding, pitch shifting, vibratos, modulating delays, and sample-and hold filters, among other effects. There are MIDI, BPM, and Tap Tempo lock functions for effect clocking. It can also do 174 seconds of mono sampling, or 87 seconds of phase-locked stereo, with looping, editing, and layering all possible.

Also available is an optional EVE/NET remote controller, which provides full functionality for control over the H8000. It features eight assignable soft-key knobs, multi-channel metering, and a joystick for panning.

Fig. 9-18: Eventide H8000

Sony DRE S-777/2

www.sony.com

Sony's DRE-S777/2 is a four-channel Impulse Response sampling reverb with 24-bit/96kHz capabilities. The DRE-S777/2 includes expansion DSP, AES/EBU digital I/O, and features an integrated LCD display. It will operate in four-channel surround or stereo modes (at 48kHz), and will do mono input to stereo output at 96kHz. There is an analog option on this unit. I have used the S777 on many

Fig. 9-19: Sony S777/2

surround projects, and the four-channel Impulse Responses are top-notch. I have also used two different stereo impulse responses, panning one set to the front and one set to the rear. Typically, I have the front decay time shorter than the surrounds, creating a nice distance effect.

Lexicon 960L

www.lexicon.com

The 960L was designed specifically for the audio, film, broadcast, post-production, and live sound markets. The software algorithms used are based upon 3D Perceptual Modeling (3DPM), developed from research into how the human brain perceives complex sounds. It features eight channels of XLR-balanced I/O (analog) and full AES/EBU I/O, all in a four-rackspace CPU mainframe. There's also an included LARC2 remote with eight touch-sensitive motorized faders, a two-axis joystick for panning, and

Fig. 9-20: Lexicon 960L

eight soft and 28 dedicated function keys. It's classic Lexicon and more, with a nice array of halls, plates, chambers, rooms, ambiences, Post Sounds, and Wild Spaces.

The many DSP configurations of this unit include Stereo, Multi-stereo (like having four classic 480Ls in one box!), 5.1 Surround, and Stereo plus 5.1 Surround. Performance is full 24-bit at resolutions up to 96kHz. Options include an Automation Package for program loads, pan moves, and parameter adjustments (synced to MIDI timecode).

There's also an optional Delays & 96kHz Reverb Package, a second Hardware DSP card to double the processing power, a second LARC2 option, an AES/EBU card, and analog I/O cards. A Multi-Channel Package is also available to enable multichannel functions and surround configurations—this also provides support for the LOGIC7 Upmix Algorithm package; users can derive multichannel surround output from stereo input sources. As always, it's best to create surround from original multitracks, but I've actually used this algorithm and it's quite impressive (especially when there are no original tapes to be found!).

TC Electronic M6000

www.tcelectronic.com

The System 6000, which is also known as a Reverb 6000 (when additional licenses are not purchased), features delays, reverbs, and effects from mono, stereo, LCR, and LtRt, through full 5.1 and 6.1 algorithms. The hardware components for System 6000 and Reverb 6000 are identical, and the Mainframe 6000 holds the DSPs and I/Os.

There are also two different types of remote controls. A touch-sensitive TC Icon remote connects to the remote CPU with a single multi-pin cable. Icon has six motorized touch-sensitive faders and an active-matrix color LCD display. The TC Icon, combined with the Remote CPU 6000, is the control interface of the Mainframe 6000.

Fig. 9-21: TC Electronic 6000

There is also a software version of the TC Icon controller for Mac and PC platforms. All functions available on the TC Icon hardware version are also available in the software editor. You only need an Ethernet connection in your Mac or PC to connect the software editor to a Mainframe.

Multiple Mainframes, hardware Icons, and software Icons can be connected in a network using Ethernet and TCP/IP protocol. Up to ten Icon control surfaces can be connected to the same Mainframe, and, for those *really* big projects, up to 254 Mainframes can be in the same network.

An optional monitor, mouse, and/or keyboard can be connected, and the system runs at sample rates up to 96kHz. The aforementioned additional licenses give the System 6000 a powerful punch for surround work.

Their newest software, Version 3.30, includes the Extended Skywalker Collection with 5.1 and 6.1 formats, additional Unwrap (TC's upmix software) capabilities, and a new "Swirl, Wave, and Psycho" effect bank for 5.1 and 6.1 formats. TC's VSS 5.1 Reverb algorithm also features multi-directional patterns and five uncorrelated reverbs, allowing for movements within the surround field. Many other optional software algorithms are available as well.

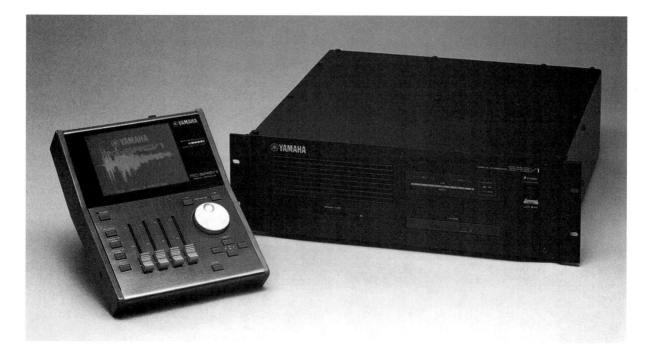

Fig. 9-22: Yamaha SREV1

Yamaha SREV1

www.yamaha.com

Yamaha's SREV1 Sampling Reverberator is another type of convolution processing reverb. It features two-channel, dual two-channel, and four-channel modes and has 79 programs on the provided CD-ROM. There's also a four-band parametric EQ for pre- and post-reverb processing, and it can be quick-switched via MIDI messages. SREV1 supports 24-bit/48kHz audio, and offers 32-bit internal processing, AES/EBU I/O, two Mini-YGDAI card slots, and an optional RC-SREV1 Remote Controller. A/D and D/A cards are available for analog I/O. For those who like to create their own sounds, it comes with measurement and Impulse Response software to sample your own acoustic environments.

Kurzweil KSP8

www.kurzweil.org

The Kurzweil KSP8 is a multi-bus signal processor featuring eight-channel operation, analog I/O, and digital I/O via AES/EBU and S/PDIF. The KSP8 has flexible signal routing, and each input signal has its own multi-band EQ and stereo or multichannel panner. There are 249 DSP algorithms which create over 600 effect presets, and the effect busses can be routed directly to the unit's outputs. Six-channel surround ambience and reverbs are included, as well as multi-channel compression. The full-blown unit can process eight separate input signals, from up to 14 different sources. Optional I/O includes four-channel analog I/O and eight channels of digital I/O via Alesis Lightpipe, mLAN (FireWire/IEEE-1394), Tascam TDIF, or AES/EBU format. Finally, there's an optional RSP8 remote control that duplicates all the controls provided by the main unit and adds a joystick and eight knobs.

CHAPTER 10

Current Surround Formats

Encoding and Decoding

Pro Tools allows you to create a multichannel audio mix, but it does not itself provide for processing in the formats described in this chapter. Format-specific encoding, which we will discuss later, must be done as a separate step, using plug-ins or external hardware.

Once a surround project is completed within Pro Tools and the final tracks are "printed," they can be delivered to the consumer in any one of several ways. In other words, from one multichannel mix, you can create a DVD, an SA-CD, a 5.1 encode for the web, or all of the above. Just realize that each will require its own specific type of file encoding, and that each will have its own set of bit rates, sample rates, and file formats to deal with. The decoding of the resulting multichannel file will take place in the end listener's playback system.

On that note, don't allow format confusion and encoding/decoding questions to hold you up—just go ahead and create your surround mix. I like to refer to this as taking a "format agnostic" approach. On occasion, especially when video is not involved, you can even decide on the specific delivery method much later in the production process.

As technology and techniques progress, it's getting easier and easier to encode and author multichannel projects for distribution. If you're not comfortable handling that end of the process, let someone with experience do it, allowing you to just focus on good content creation.

DVD-Video (DVD-V)

DVD-Video (DVD-V) can carry up to eight channels of audio, with a six-channel surround mix and a separate two-channel stereo mix (including full video content, menus, etc.). However, the audio must be encoded for playback through decoders in consumer receivers. Encoding audio files makes their size smaller, and therefore, more information can fit on a disc. Certain DVD players have decoders built in, so you don't always have to rely on the receiver.

Dolby Digital, which is also referred to as AC-3, is a standard for the DVD-V format, encoded at up to 448 kbps at a maximum resolution of 24 bits/48kHz. You shouldn't think of Dolby Digital encoding as 5.1 only, since you can also include a Dolby Digital stereo (2.0) mix on a disc, in addition to the multichannel tracks. Another option for DVD-V is the inclusion of a DTS layer, which can be encoded at up to 1,536 kbps at 24-bit/96kHz. Note that both DTS and Dolby also have playback capabilities beyond six channels, but we'll get to that later. As you can see, it makes sense to capture and/or mix your tracks at the highest resolution possible, even though your audio will be compressed for final delivery. Better to have high-resolution audio and down-sample it than to not have it at all!

Some of the benefits of DVD-V include:

- Full 5.1 surround sound with Dolby Digital and/or DTS encoded tracks.

- Can include multiple streams of audio data, including compressed MPEG or uncompressed PCM types.

- Full video content, with some discs even offering different camera angles.

- Most successful consumer electronics product in history.

- Room on the disc for "bonus" sections, such as artist interviews and additional tracks (since encoded audio takes up less space than non-encoded audio).

- Plays back in any of the over 54 million DVD players in existence today.

- Can carry 6.1 formats as well.

- Most DVD-V titles are DVD-5 and DVD-9 discs. (See DVD Format Chart below.)

Some examples of music-oriented DVD-V discs on the market today:

- The Eagles—*Hell Freezes Over*

- U2—*Elevated Tour*

- The Beatles—*The Beatles Anthology*

- Slipknot—*Disasterpieces*

- Carly Simon—*Live from Martha's Vineyard*

DVD Format Chart

Disc Type	GB	Sides	Layers
DVD-5	4.7	1	1
DVD-9	8.54	1	2
DVD-10	9.4	2	1
DVD-18	17.08	2	2

PRO TOOLS SURROUND SOUND MIXING

DVD-Audio (DVD-A)

DVD-Audio (DVD-A) discs offer additional musical appeal in that they can contain six channels of high-resolution 88.2 or 96kHz/24-bit unencoded PCM audio, as well as a high-resolution stereo mix. Overall, the focus of this format is on its audio capabilities. DVD-A uses an optional encoding scheme called MLP (Meridian Lossless Packing), which allows up to eight channels of hi-res audio to fit on the disc. It also can contain a 5.1 DTS 96/24 layer and a 96/24 stereo re-mastered track for DVD-V compatibility. The DVD-Audio spec even provides for the option of including two channels of 192kHz audio (a good reason to have Pro Tools HD!).

DVD-A does not offer the video capability of DVD-V, and you also must have a DVD-Audio or a "universal" player to play the disc. Certain models of new cars now offer full surround with DVD-A playback. Even though it's a music-driven format, it is currently more challenging to author a DVD-A disc than its DVD-V cousin.

Some benefits of DVD-A:

- Higher resolution audio capabilities than DVD-V.

- The optional video zone of the DVD-A disc can contain Dolby Digital, DTS, or stereo PCM layers for DVD-V playback.

- Some artists prefer the format for its focus on audio.

- Certain models of cars have DVD-A players with full surround playback.

Some examples of DVD-A discs on the market:

- Queen—*Bohemian Rhapsody*

- Fleetwood Mac—*Rumors*

- REM—*Document*

- Neil Young—*Harvest*

SA-CD (Super Audio Compact Disc)

"SA-CD" stands for Super Audio Compact Disc and was jointly created by Sony and Phillips. On first appearance, an SA-CD looks like any classic 12-cm-diameter, 1.2-mm-thick optical disc. Inside, though, the storage capability is tremendous. A single-layer disc can hold 4.7GB of data, with a multi-layer disc holding almost 9GB.

In the same way that most of the digital audio we work on today uses PCM (Pulse Code Modulation) technology for data storage, SA-CD utilizes DSD (Direct Stream Digital) technology. DSD is based on 1-bit sigma-delta modulation with a sample rate of 2.8224 million times a second, which is 64 times the amount of astandard CD. Actually, DSD was originally developed for archiving analog master tapes. SA-CD is therefore based upon a totally different technology than the CD or DVD, which use PCM (already defined above) data.

SA-CD supports several disc configurations, including a Hybrid design which is compatible with the millions of standard CD players in the market today. Hybrid SA-CDs contain two complete layers of music information: One layer contains the high-density DSD recording that can be played in the new generations of stereo and surround SA-CD players, and the other is a conventional two-channel Red Book CD layer, playable on any standard CD player. Some SA-CD titles without surround simply contain a two-channel DSD layer and a Red Book CD layer.

SA-CD uses DST (Direct Stream Transfer) lossless data compression for DSD data. DST is used to:

- Increase the effective data transfer rate from the disk, required for multichannel streams.

- Increase the data capacity of the disc.

DST may also be optionally used on the stereo stream. All SA-CD players decode DST-encoded data on the fly. Data compression (packing) of up to 50% is possible, depending on the program material.

Some benefits of SA-CD:

- Can carry a six-channel high-resolution mix, a two-channel hi-res mix, and a 16-bit Red Book CD mix, all on the same disc.

- Stereo 16-bit Red Book layer will play back on any CD player.

- Also being used as a format to capture stereo PCM masters.

- No video monitor needed for playback.

Some examples of SA-CDs currently on the market:

- Pink Floyd—*Dark Side of the Moon*

- Alice In Chains—*Greatest Hits*

- Tony Bennett—*Playin' with my Friends*

- James Taylor—*JT*

Encoded CD

This format takes a DTS encoded track (up to 5.1 channels) and places it on a standard CD, up to a maximum of 74 minutes. However, you need to have a S/PDIF digital out connection from your player to a receiver with DTS decoding capabilities, or have the player itself provide the DTS decoding; otherwise, a very unpleasant noise will be heard. The bit rate of a DTS encoded CD is 1.235 Mbps.

WMA 9

WMA 9 is shorthand for Microsoft's Windows Media Audio 9 Series of codecs (coder/decoders), which allow for up to 7.1 (eight) channels of audio with full support for up to 24-bit/96kHz data. In this "Series," different encoder types each have their own purpose—for high-resolution stereo and multichannel audio, you would use the Windows Media Audio 9 Professional codec. This surround sound codec can create content suitable for streaming over the web, delivered at data rates ranging from 128-768 kbps.

Encoding with the Professional codec is a lossy method of encoding, but there is also a lossless codec called Windows Media Audio 9 Lossless. It can compress audio at a 2:1–3:1 ratio, with no loss in quality. The downside is that the data rates are much higher, which may be much too high for streaming. However, the Lossless codec is perfect for archiving digital sources. Check out this website and download the free player: http://www.microsoft.com/windows/windowsmedia/default.aspx

WMA 9 can also be used to play back 5.1 audio over your PC, provided you have a surround-capable card. Note that Windows Media Player 10 is in beta at the time of the writing of this book.

WMA 9 potential applications include:

- Streaming your surround mixes over the web.

- Live encoding and broadcasting.

- PC surround playback.

- Satellite broadcasting.

- Multiple bit rate (MBR) streaming.

- Delivery on CD or DVD.

The Most Common Formats for Encoding Surround Material

Dolby Digital

Also known as AC-3, Dolby Digital is a type of audio compression that provides up to 5.1 channels of discrete audio, delivered over a single stream. It uses a constant-bit-rate (CBR) data stream that groups frequency values into varying widths matched to critical bands of our hearing. Each block of values is then converted into a floating-point representation of frequency, which is allocated a varying number of bits according to the importance of the bands.

AC-3 is a lossy perceptual coding method, meaning that data is lost in the encoding stage. Supported sampling rates include 32, 44.1, and 48kHz, although 48kHz is required for DVDs. The variable bit rates range from 32 kbps (mono) up to 640 kbps. Since Dolby Digital is a mandatory format for inclusion on DVD-V discs, many projects encode at the 384 kbps rate, although you certainly can use the maximum rate of 448 kbps. DVD-A discs often have a Dolby Digital encoded track as an option.

Dolby Digital decoders can downmix surround sound material into matrixed Dolby Pro Logic, or into stereo, or mono. Also, many projects include a stereo Dolby

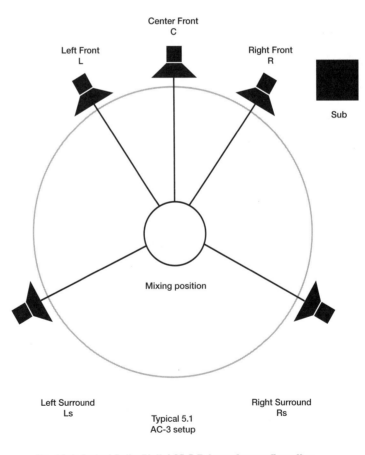

Fig. 10-1: Typical Dolby Digital AC-3 5.1 speaker configuration

Digital mix, not only for compatibility with non-surround playback systems, but to save valuable disc space.

Common formats that use Dolby Digital include:

- DVD-Video.

- HDTV broadcast.

- Motion pictures.

- DVD-Audio bonus tracks.

- Games that play back through the Microsoft X-Box or a surround-ready PC.

Dolby EX

Dolby EX is a 6.1 Dolby format that adds an extra Rear Center channel. The configuration is: Front Left, Center, Right, Rear Right, Center, Left, LFE. A receiver with Dolby EX decoding is required to play back this format. However, since the Rear Center signal is matrix-encoded into the Rear Left and Right channels, a Dolby EX surround mix will play back normally if EX (or THX Surround EX) decoding is not present, or if a Rear Center speaker is not connected.

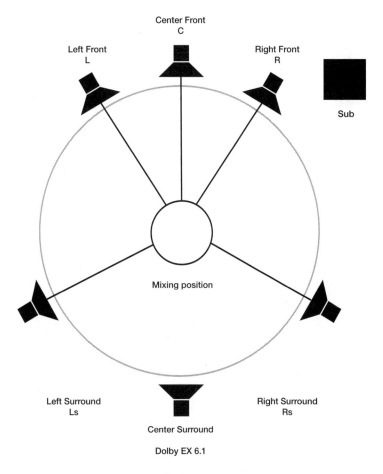

Fig. 10-2: Dolby EX speaker setup

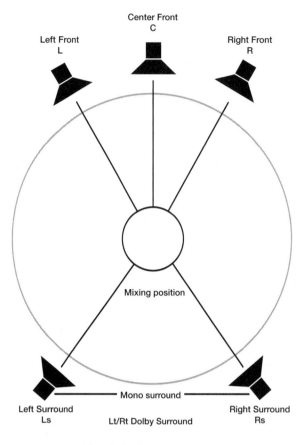

Center Front
C

Left Front
L

Right Front
R

Mixing position

Mono surround

Left Surround
Ls

Right Surround
Rs

Lt/Rt Dolby Surround

Fig. 10-3: Dolby Surround speaker setup

Dolby Surround

This is a phase-matrix process that allows any stereo medium to carry four channels of audio, regardless of whether it is an analog or digital signal. Often called an Lt/Rt (Left Total, Right Total) signal, when sent through a Dolby Pro Logic decoder, four channels of audio will be re-created from stereo: Left, Center, Right, and Surround (bandwidth-limited mono). Pro Logic decoding relies on phase and amplitude differences between the two Lt/Rt channels to extract the four-channel mix. Dolby Surround, which was originally developed as a sound-for-picture format, is totally compatible with both mono and stereo playback. A consumer listening at home without Pro Logic decoding will hear the mono or stereo mix normally, while those with the decoder will get the surround experience. A description of the Dolby Surround plug-in for Pro Tools is presented in Chapter 9.

Dolby Pro Logic II

This is an enhanced version of Dolby Pro Logic that allows for the matrix encoding of five channels of audio into an Lt/Rt signal. These five channels (Left, Center, Right, Left Surround, and Right Surround) are full bandwidth, unlike Pro Logic. The steering algorithms in Pro Logic II reproduce surround audio much more accu-

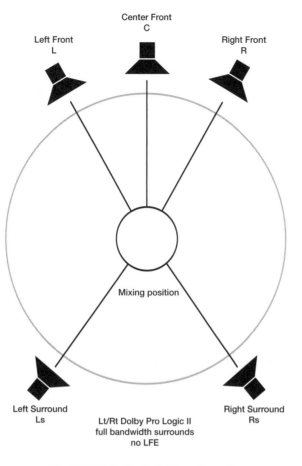

Left Front
L

Center Front
C

Right Front
R

Mixing position

Left Surround
Ls

Right Surround
Rs

Lt/Rt Dolby Pro Logic II
full bandwidth surrounds
no LFE

Fig. 10-4: Dolby Pro Logic II speaker setup

rately than Pro Logic. Note that Pro Logic and Pro Logic II don't carry any LFE
information.

Dolby E

Dolby E is designed primarily for multichannel broadcast through a two-channel
infrastructure. It allows a single digital AES3 pair to carry up to eight channels of
audio, plus Dolby Digital metadata. Unlike Dolby Digital or PL encodes, Dolby E
can withstand up to ten encode/decode cycles, making it a very robust medium.
Also, Dolby E frames match video frames, allowing for easy editing. It can handle
transfers through satellites (for example, when a network sends an E-encoded program to its affiliates).

Dolby manufactures the DP571 Dolby E Encoder, which accepts up to eight
channels of digital audio and Dolby Digital metadata, outputting a Dolby E-encoded
AES3 bitstream that can be transmitted through a two-channel broadcast network.
The DP572 Dolby E Decoder takes that AES3 signal and outputs up to eight channels of audio, along with the Dolby Digital metadata. Note that there are no consumer Dolby E decoders—its uses are for professional broadcast and audio
distribution only.

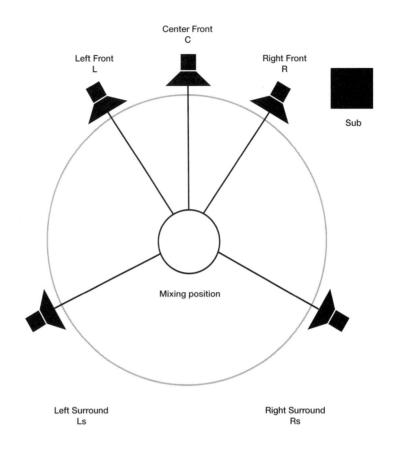

Fig. 10-5: Typical DTS 5.1 speaker configuration

DTS

DTS Digital Surround is also a lossy encoding method. It supports up to eight channels of audio, at rates of up to 24-bit/96kHz. DTS features a higher data rate than Dolby Digital: either 1.509 Mbps or the half-rate of 754 kbps (often used where space is limited on the disc). However, this doesn't mean it sounds better based upon data rate alone; it simply uses a different technology than Dolby does. It is an option to include a DTS track on both DVD-V and DVD-A discs, and some producers do prefer its sonic qualities.

Common formats that use DTS:

- DVD-Video and DVD-Audio (both as an option).

- Motion pictures.

- Video games.

- DTS-encoded CDs.

- Laser Discs (yes, there are some still around!).

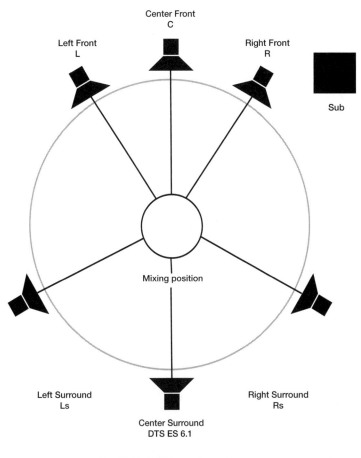

Center Front
C

Left Front
L

Right Front
R

Sub

Mixing position

Left Surround
Ls

Right Surround
Rs

Center Surround
DTS ES 6.1

Fig. 10-6: DTS ES speaker setup

DTS ES

DTS ES (Extended Surround) is a discrete 6.1 format that also adds an extra Rear Center channel (Cs) to a 5.1 mix. It encodes the 6.1 input (L, C, R, Ls, Cs, Rs, LFE) to provide a discrete 6.1 bitstream as well as a 5.1 downmixed bitstream. It is backwards-compatible with existing decoders, and is also compatible with 5.1 decoders, 5.1 decoders plus matrix decoders, and discrete 6.1 decoders. In other words, if a 5.1 decoder sees the bitstream, it will produce a phantom center surround, heard between the Left and Right Surrounds. A 5.1 decoder with matrix derives the Cs channel from the matrix decoder itself. A 6.1 discrete decoder produces discrete Ls, Cs, and Rs channels.

SRS Labs Circle Surround

SRS Circle Surround is an encode/decode system that can provide up to 6.1 channels of surround sound from a two-channel track. Circle Surround is 100% mono and stereo compatible, so people without a surround receiver will simply hear a standard mix, or even an enhanced stereo mix. Those with a decoder such as Dolby

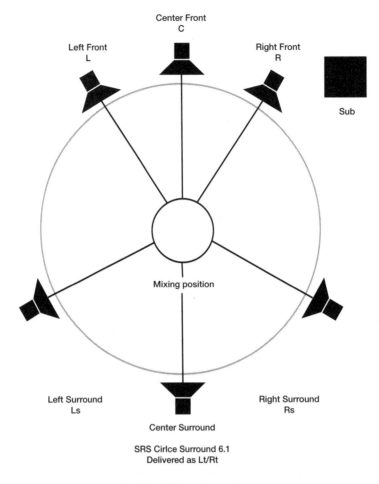

Center Front
C

Left Front
L

Right Front
R

Sub

Mixing position

Left Surround
Ls

Right Surround
Rs

Center Surround

SRS Cirlce Surround 6.1
Delivered as Lt/Rt

Fig. 10-7: SRS speaker setup

Pro Logic, Pro Logic II, or DTS Neo 6 will hear a surround mix. Since it's deliverable over a standard stereo medium, Circle Surround has been used by networks like ESPN, ABC, NBC, CBS, and others, and is now appearing on DVD-V tracks; there are even Circle Surround-encoded music CDs.

To produce a track in SRS Circle Surround, simply take your 5.1 or 6.1 mix and send it through the Circle Surround TDM encoder plug-in. The plug-in will then take the Front channels, Center channel, LFE channel, and Surrounds, and output a stereo-compatible two-channel Lt/Rt mix. That mix can then be printed onto any platform you want, including a standard audio CD. You can check the results of the processing within Pro Tools by using the plug-in's Circle Surround Decoder. Descriptions of the SRS Circle Surround TDM PRO plug-ins are provided in Chapter 9.

Some benefits of encoding surround material with SRS Circle Surround:

- A standard analog RCA jack can carry surround signal.

- Up to 6.1 surround from a two-channel track.

- Can deliver surround over such media as radio, television, online distribution, CD, and/or DVD.

- Great added value for a CD or DVD project.

- Can be encoded and decoded all inside Pro Tools.

MLP

MLP, or Meridian Lossless Packing, is actually a mathematical encoding technique that compresses audio bit-for bit without discarding any data. MLP is used to reduce data rates in order to fit into that 9.6 Mbps data pipe. In order to achieve its almost 2:1 compression ratio, MLP uses lossless matrixing, lossless waveform prediction, and entropy coding. Along with the multichannel mix, MLP can encode a two-channel downmix, as well as carry additional information such as text, timecodes, and dynamic range control profiles. Just remember that MLP has no effect on the audio.

What Is THX?

THX is not a format for encoding audio. Primarily, it's a trademark used to identify a theater's compliance with the Lucasfilm THX requirements for their sound system and acoustics. Also, the THX logo is often seen on home theater components, which identifies that the product complies with the aforementioned Lucasfilm THX standards. Think of it as a seal of quality that helps ensure proper reproduction of surround audio. You'll also soon start seeing THX certifications in vehicles, known as the THX Certified Car Audio program.

Overall

As mentioned, both Dolby Digital and DTS are lossy encoding schemes that result in discarded audio data, whereas MLP and DST (used solely in SA-CD) don't lose any information at all. For the lossy encoding schemes, always try to use the higher data rates, thus increasing audio quality, while keeping an eye on your project's "bit budget." (For an explanation of bit budgeting, see the case study in Chapter 6.) Since encoding doesn't take that long on today's speedy computers, you can experiment by trying various data rates to see which one works best for your particular application.

It also helps to think ahead when capturing projects for surround. The next wave of technology is already on the horizon (see below), which should bring the capability of full multichannel playback at high bit and sample rates. So don't worry that not everyone can hear your beautiful 96kHz 6.1 mixes just yet. Before you know it, you'll be doing a total recall to deliver a full-resolution mix to the record company—and you'll be glad you recorded and mixed it that way to begin with.

So What Format Do You Choose?

There's no simple answer to this question. I like to think of it this way: If you have a six-channel master, you can go any way you choose, but certain additional factors will guide your decision. If you have video accompanying your audio, DVD-V probably makes the most sense, due to the fact that it's a hot medium with millions of consumers actually seeking product. If you have hi-res PCM audio without video, DVD-A may be your best bet. You could also choose to send your PCM audio through converters to create DSD tracks for an SA-CD. Some labels, such as Telarc, are actually capturing straight to DSD, but you need the proper equipment to do this.

As to what type of encoded audio to use, and at what resolutions, that is a choice of the producer, artist, and/or record company, and is often a function of the physical space allocations on each disc. An additional factor is how the actual project was recorded. Some of the older analog masters that are being remixed are first transferred to high-resolution hard-disk workstations such as Pro Tools for their multichannel makeover. Other projects, mostly newer recordings, can be captured directly to disk at resolutions up to 192kHz.

Several next-generation, high-definition formats are currently in the works. Even though each has its benefits, the last thing consumers need is more confusion. Having said that, technology will always march onwards—so here's a chart of what each one offers. Only time will tell which is ultimately released and accepted.

Blu-Ray Disc

- Endorsed by over 13 major PC and consumer electronics companies, including Hitachi, Matsushita, Pioneer, Samsung, Sharp, and Sony.

- Disc will be housed in a protective cartridge.

- Disc has over 25GB of storage on the single-layer disc, 50GB on the double.

- Advanced copy protection.

- High-speed transfer data rate of 36 Mbps.

- HD picture and audio.

- Broadband connectivity.

- Interactive features.

Toshiba/NEC HD DVD

- Features HD picture and hi-def audio.

- Manufacturing is switchable with current DVD lines (very important!).

- Advanced copy protection.

- Backwards compatibility with PCs and consumer electronics devices.

- Internet connectivity.

- Interactive features.

Case Study: How Your Surround Mixes Are Heard Through a Consumer Receiver/Home Theater

The truth is that a large percentage of surround mixes will be heard in the home theater environment. Due to the massive acceptance of the DVD-Video platform and the low prices on HTIB (Home Theater in a Box) setups, consumers by the millions can now easily hear your work. Just as the computer is the nerve center of your Pro Tools setup, the consumer receiver is the brain of most home surround setups.

Let's take a look at one of the latest models of these consumer receivers: the Lexicon RV-8. To help us examine how it handles the various multichannel audio

Fig. 10-8: Front of Lexicon Receiver

Fig. 10-9: Back of Lexicon Receiver

streams, I asked Andrew Clark, Vice President of Marketing for the Harman Specialty Group, a few questions about the important functions of the RV-8.

Interview with Andrew Clark from Lexicon

Q: How does the RV-8 play back the following multichannel sources: DVD-Audio and SA-CD?

A: DVD-Audio and SA-CD are treated in the same manner. Prior to entering the RV-8 input, the signals are converted from digital to analog in the disc player and output as a 5.1-channel analog signal. The RV-8 then accepts that analog input; then one of two things happens, depending on how the user has set up the RV-8 to handle it.

One option is to send the 5.1-channel analog signal to the internal level controls (also known as "analog bypass"), then to the amplifier for output to the speakers. This allows the signal to remain in the analog domain, but does not allow for bass management or other types of processing. This puts the burden of bass management on the disc player, and implementation of bass management in disc players has traditionally been minimalist and inconsistent.

The other option is to convert the 5.1-channel analog signal into a digital signal in the RV-8 so the user can utilize comprehensive bass management and other processing to better suit their speaker setup and listening preferences.

Critics would argue that the downside of this approach is that the signal undergoes two additional stages of conversion: digital to analog in the disc player and analog to digital in the RV-8. Until the industry finally settles on a high-resolution digital link standard between DVD-A and SA-CD players and receivers and preamp/processors, users will have to decide what method they prefer.

Q: How does the RV-8 play back DVD-V, either DTS or Dolby?

A: These are treated a little differently, since they are "compressed" audio formats and the content providers are much less concerned about allowing these signals to be sent via the *digital* audio outputs of the disc players. However, these signals can carry a wide range of configurations from mono to 6.1 channels. Inside the RV-8, these signals can be played in the unaltered form, or processing can be applied to make them utilize all of the speakers in the system. We have found that most enthusiasts are utilizing 7.1 channels for playback if their room layout can support it.

Q: How does it handle bass management of the incoming surround audio?

A: Bass management in the RV-8 is completely driven by the speaker selections the user has made. By selecting the frequencies that each speaker can accommodate, the low frequencies are directed to the speakers that are most capable of reproducing them. For instance, if a system has two full-range front Left and Right speakers, a restricted-low-frequency Center channel, and surround speakers, then the low frequencies from the Center channel and surround speakers will be re-directed to the front Left and Right speakers. If the system is using restricted-frequency front Left and Right speakers as well, the low frequencies will be sent to the subwoofer output. The goal of comprehensive bass management is to make sure that no signals get "thrown away" and that the speakers that are least capable of reproducing low frequencies are protected from them.

Q: How does the receiver create fold-downs of a surround mix?

A: It utilizes a proprietary Logic7 encoding process to create a fold-down that, when played back through Logic7, sounds very close to the original surround mix—even in stereo. We put in a lot of effort to get this right. The nice thing about a Logic7-encoded mix is that it also retains compatibility with other matrix decoders such as Dolby Pro Logic.

Q: How does Logic7 unfold a stereo source into a 7.1 listening experience?

A: It first looks at the signal to decide if it is matrix encoded or not. If it sees hallmarks of matrix encoding, it applies steering to reproduce the steering and surround events as the mixer intended. If it does not detect matrix encoding, it relies on the ambience contained in the recording to utilize all of the speakers in the system to create a more enveloping surround field. It is important to note that it does not add sounds that are not part of the original recording; it just directs the sounds that are in the recording to the speakers that are best able to convey a stronger sense of a real space. For instance, Logic7 will carefully distribute the reverberation in a recording in the surround channels to mimic the reverberation in a real space. This gives the listener a deeper sensation that they are in the "room" with the musicians.

Q: What is THX Ultra2 and THX Surround EX decoding? Are they encoded formats that need decoding?

A: As far as a receiver is concerned, THX Ultra2 is two things. It is a certification program that ensures that a product with this logo has met all of the performance criteria that Home THX has established for proper playback of music and film in the home. And it is also a set of features and digital processes for the playback of music and films in the home.

I won't go into detail here, but the basic intent of the processes is to reproduce film soundtracks and musical recordings (whether they are mono, stereo, or multi-channel) in the home as the director or musicians intended. "THX Surround EX," also known as "Dolby Digital EX" or simply "EX," was an enhancement added to 5.1-channel soundtracks to create a surround Rear channel (also known as "6.1").

Since 5.1-channel soundtracks utilize stereo surround channels, it was a simple process to add matrix encoding (Dolby Pro Logic, for example) to the surround channels. Then, when played back through an "EX" decoder, a Center Surround channel would be extracted. This clever use of existing technologies allows for backward compatibility with 5.1-channel systems, while providing a better sound experience for users with 6.1 channels in their system. This has since become the standard configuration in most mid- and high-end electronics.

CHAPTER 11

Additional Outlets for Surround Sound

The Concepts Are Generally the Same

The surround functionality of Pro Tools has many applications. From 5.1 music mixes for DVD-Video and DVD-Audio to a four-channel sound bed for the latest game, it can easily handle the job. Certainly, the post-production world—including both film and television—relies heavily on the latest multichannel technologies Pro Tools delivers.

No matter what field you mix for, the concepts of surround sound remain the same. Certainly each medium has its own specific requirements and delivery needs, but once you grasp the big picture, the details become much easier to achieve.

Below are a few informative interviews with professionals who use Pro Tools to create multichannel projects for game and commercial production.

Surround Game Production

Clint Bajakian knows a thing or two about audio for games. After spending nine years as a sound-design supervisor at Lucas Arts Entertainment, he joined forces with sound designer Julian Kwasneski to form Bay Area Sound Department (BASD) in 2000. Between them, they collectively have over 20 years of experience and have worked on over 70 game titles. I asked Clint a few questions to help bring some insight into the art of audio for games.

Q: What titles have you been working on lately?

A: We've been getting a lot of high-caliber sound-design jobs, including sound effects for Blizzard's *StarCraft: Ghost, Lord of the Rings Return of the King,* and *James Bond, Everything or Nothing,* for Electronic Arts.

Fig. 11-1: Clint Bajakian

Last year I worked on *Indiana Jones and the Emperor's Tomb* for LucasArts, which used a live orchestra. We used the Northwest Sinfonia, recorded by Steve Smith at a Bastyr chapel. He set up a mobile guerrilla recording rig with full 5.0 Decca Tree, close mics, and ambient mics. That was the first project that Lucas Arts ever hired a live orchestra for.

Q: Since this was for a game, how was it captured for surround sound?

A: Steve Smith set up a Decca Tree that was about eight feet back from the conductor and about 30 feet wide. Three large-diaphragm high-quality condensor mics were used for the L, C, R (Left, Center, Right). Then he had two high B&K omni ambient mics about 30 feet back, 20 feet up in the air, and about 30 feet apart. Zooming ahead to post, orchestrator Steve Zuckerman, who had a lot of experience, helped us get a great orchestral sound. Steve said, "It's not about the mix in post, it's about the sound you capture at the date," at that recording session. You can't fix it in the mix.

Q: How did the surround tracks help the overall mix in Pro Tools?

A: We found that the Decca Tree sounded amazing but it really came alive when we brought up those surround microphones in the rear speakers. I discretely assigned each room microphone to the corresponding speakers: Left Surround and Right Surround. We used spot and close mics for emphasis. Interestingly, you can almost erode the purity with the close mics, so you keep them low.

Q: What is so difficult about using surround for a game, in comparison with a movie?

A: In a film, there is a mixing session where the entire mix can be committed to six channels or more, in a linear format that plays back the same way every time. In a game, there are two requirements: First, the game is interactive, so you can't lock all the elements together—you don't know when the gun is going to fire and you don't know when the plane will fly by the camera. There are a lot of real-time elements. Also, you don't know the camera's relationship to various environmental features. For example, with a waterfall—in a film, if the character and the camera turn, the location of the waterfall shifts in the background ambience. That can be panned and accommodated. In a game, you don't know when the player will move left or right or turn the main character. The game player could just have that character do a continuous 360 just for fun, and that waterfall goes around and around.

Second is the nature of the game hardware and the audio playback system. Some game platforms, in terms of the consoles for TV and the PC, are more easily translated into 5.1 surround. The main consoles are Microsoft XBox, Sony PlayStation2, and Nintendo GameCube, but the PC is also making a re-emergence. Of those primary three, there was a design built into the XBox (a strategic relationship between Microsoft and Dolby Labs) that led to a real-time encode of what is essentially an AC-3 bitstream.

The big thing they overcame was the processing time. It takes time to process and encode six channels of audio to a bitstream and send it out to a decoder. It also takes a little bit of time for that decoder to decode the audio. Here you are pushing the trigger on your gun, and if that has to go through an encode/decode process, you could be as many as 150 milliseconds late. They got it down to an incredibly impressive number, and it's primarily done on a super-powerful nVidea chip.

Q: So these platforms all have 5.1 capabilities?

A: The PlayStation2 has 5.1 capabilities, but most of the processing has to be done in software. The XBox has a real-time Dolby Digital 5.1 surround encode process built into the hardware. That means all the multichannel surround information gets encoded to that digital bitstream and sent out the digital output to the consumer decoder in real time, "for free." That expression, "for free," means it doesn't cost any system resources, especially the main processor, which is busy drawing polygons and updating environmental features. That main processor is basically being consumed quite heavily by art, graphic, and game-play processing. All that stuff is completely untouched by the surround audio, and that's a very exciting aspect of the XBox hardware.

Q: How is Dolby surround used in games?

A: Sony's PlayStation2 has powerful central sound processing to handle the 5.1 surround. However, there is something else that is even more practical for systems that don't have real-time "for free" system-independent 5.1 encode—it's Dolby Pro Logic II surround technology. Dolby's PL II, which still is just a stereo delivery, can create discrete surround—or the illusion of it. A two-channel Pro Logic II encoded signal, decoded with a PL II decoder, will unfold just stunningly close to the original, discrete four-channel source.

That becomes unbelievably powerful in the world of games. The reason is that there are system limitations on most game platforms, including XBox. Maybe the 5.1 comes "for free," but other things don't. It takes system processing power to accomplish most anything.

To have a simple stereo file that is decoded on the consumer side in the home theater and is unfolded to 5.0 (PL II doesn't support LFE) surround is just stunning, and it's amazingly resource-effective.

Q: How do you use your Pro Tools setup in surround?

A: We use Pro Tools for the mixing and scoring, usually directly to video using QuickTime. You do your project as a conventional multichannel mix with multiple bus outputs. If it's quad, you obviously have four master channel outputs. If it's 5.0, you have five, and if it's 5.1 you have six of them. It's important to remember that the LFE gets ignored with Pro Logic II. You then route those four or five channels to a Pro Logic II encoder.

Q: How do you run audio into the encoder from Pro Tools?

A: Your AES/EBU outputs from Pro Tools go into the Dolby hardware encoder, and it echoes the audio unaltered to three outputs (three AES/EBU channels), which are fed into my digital mixer. It just passes through unaltered if I'm working discretely, as the PL II encoder just sits in the chain. But it also has a single AES/EBU output, out of which streams the encoded audio signal. In my case, I route it right back into Pro Tools, and I can monitor that one stereo channel and send it as an aux send from my mixer to a consumer decoder.

Then, when I switch back and forth between the multichannel playback directly from Pro Tools, and I mute those four to six channels and unmute the PL II encoded stream, I can listen to that encoded stereo signal and hear what arguably most people are going to hear—which is just a stereo playback on their stereo system. Little do they know, however, that it's an encoded format!

That signal then gets sent to a decoder over an aux send, so if I do it pre-fader, I can mute the faders on the mixer and cease listening to the signal directly from the Pro Logic II encoder. I can then bring up multichannel inputs on the mixer, coming from the decoder. Now I'm listening to the decoded multichannel signal, over the exact same speakers.

If you calibrate your speakers so the listening level is roughly the same, you can go back and forth from a discrete CD-quality source (where it's all discrete channels in Pro Tools), mute those, and unmute the same channels coming from the consumer decoder to hear the difference between the whole process. It's stunning how close the two are when you hear them like that. Then you can check for mono compatibility.

Q: So what is the benefit of encoded stereo delivery for games?

A: The beauty of it for games is that you are only costing the development team and the game platform system the overhead of dealing with stereo files. People with a decoder can then get surround.

Because of all that, it really doesn't make sense not to encode as a matter of course, especially sound ambiences, because it's just "for free." Why not encode it, because if most people are going to play it over stereo, that's just fine. But if they do have a decoder, even a Pro Logic one, they will get a surround experience, because it's backwards compatible.

The other thing is, this audio will decode to surround whether it's playing from a Game Cube, a PlayStation2, an XBox, or even an iPod. A PL II–encoded stereo file will play from anything that's capable of playing a stereo file, and even at lower sample rates, it tends not to degrade the effect of the encode too much. You can even compress and EQ the signal; it's very durable. You can convert it to different formats like MP3 and it will still be unfolded to a surround mix.

Q: How does the game get assembled once you deliver elements out of Pro Tools?

A: The three main dramatic elements in the audio are D,M, and E: Dialog, Music, and Effects. That's true in film, TV, or anything with picture.

In terms of the dialog, the files ship on the disc as separate mono files. They usually get streamed, because a dialog line could be anywhere from one second to 15 seconds. So it's generally not practical to load them into memory. Since they are streamed in real time, because you don't know when they will be needed, they have to remain separate, discrete files on disc. Those files, ideally, according to film practice, should play over the Center channel. So for the XBox, there is the provision to play back dialog to the Center speaker, and I think that's where we're headed with all game platforms.

Sound effects vary between being mono and stereo assets. In some cases, you have multichannel sound-effect assets, generally for things like ambience. It's possible that, for a game, those will actually consist of two stereo files—a Left/Right Front and a Left Surround/Right Surround, or even four mono files, each assigned to one of those four discrete quad speakers.

However, those are rare. What's more common is for the ambience to be a Dolby Pro Logic II–encoded stereo file that gets decoded to surround. Certainly, it's cool to have a discrete multichannel source that gets streamed, but it just takes up more resources—simply more data coming off the disc.

For sound effects, certainly action ones that are events onscreen, there are some that are stereo. But in general, they have to be mono, ironically, to deliver a surround experience. This is because, around ten years ago, they developed technology that uses HRTF (Head Related Transfer Function) algorithms to simulate a three-dimensional placement of a sound source. So if you had a helicopter flying around your head, you could sit in front of a stereo system, and it would fly around you. The algorithms have improved, and the "color" is now much better.

Your fantastic explosions, cars, and guns have to be mono in order to come out in surround, because they are being steered as a mono file in real time with those HRTF functions.

Q: How about music?

A: Music for games, generally speaking, is still produced in stereo, and normally ships in stereo. There are some exceptions, especially in live recording, such as the Indiana Jones game, where the whole original source was recorded and mixed in surround.

However, you could create a surround effect in your studio and use surround panning, then encode it to Pro Logic II, or Pro Logic. Again, it's a stereo file, but the surround comes "for free" for those who have decoders. Now, the trick that can be done, either in real time or in post-production, is to take a conventional stereo music file, send it to a reverb, and then send the reverb only to the surrounds. You would then attenuate it 6 to 10dB. This way, it just sort of surrounds the person. Also, you could also just mult it into the surrounds, so you feel the room presence in the surrounds.

That's often used to great effect in games. In the game, there's also the option of onboard reverb, which can be used for environments. There are two types of reverb in a game generally: the environmental ones to simulate the environment you're in, which is basically a reverb for realism, and one that's for the music potentially, which is used to make the music sound better.

It's exciting that there are now higher budgets in games and a much bigger concern for quality. Most publishers have been bitten by the bug, so it's a good time to be working on games, especially in surround!

Check out the Bay Area Sound Department at www.basound.com

Commercial Production in Surround

Hank Neuberger is a Grammy-winning producer/engineer who serves as a supervisor of Broadcast Audio for the Grammy telecast. His recent projects include recording, mixing, and/or DVD authoring for John Mayer, Ben Harper, the Roots, Flaming Lips, Anthrax, Guster, Fleetwood Mac, Michael McDonald, Cheap Trick, and Tom Petty.

An early adopter of 5.1 surround audio, Hank built one of the first DVD authoring suites in the Midwest in 1997, and produces and directs recording and DVD projects today for Third Wave Productions. He is the Executive Vice President of Chicago Recording Company, and Glenwood Place Studios in Burbank, California.

Q: What approach with surround would be typical, if any, for a commercial?

A: Commercials are a little different. What is critical is to see if the surround mix folds down to stereo and mono appropriately. In certain instances, we found that the original mixers had mixed more in the style for discrete, and you can't be quite that radical when your target is matrix encoding. So we had to go back and get the Pro Tools session file. We could then mount it effortlessly, making some minor panning adjustments by pulling some things that were all the way on the back plane up a little bit, so that when they folded down to stereo they were still an appropriate part of the mix. That was one great application of being able to hand off Pro Tools session files for commercials.

Q: Is your surround mixing all done within the Pro Tools environment, and what computers are you working on?

A: Yes, we do it all in the box. We've been running Pro Tools HD for the last year on G5s in our home facility, although we also run XP since the files have worked flawlessly. We use Accel cards running Version 6.4. The way we work today, we could not have done the projects we do just two years ago; they just weren't possible. The advent of faster processors in the computers—XPs and G5s—is a dramatic upgrade within our workflow and productivity. The new computers paid for themselves within weeks. Adding Accel cards also makes a dramatic difference. With the Anthrax DVD we had a single Pro Tools file that was 80 tracks deep and 90 minutes long. When you mix to picture like we did, it's very helpful that it's all in one session file, as opposed to trying to assemble it from a bunch of sessions, having to open and close them, resync, etc. The workflow and productivity benefits increase substantially from having it all in that one session file.

The thing about Pro Tools—and this is critical for surround—is that it's hard enough in stereo to do recalls and revisions. In surround, without a digital desk or Pro Tools, it's just impossible. You would have to go back to the original studio, get the original gear, get the original assistant—since he or she took the original notes to begin with—and then maybe you get just close. In Pro Tools, all I carry is a FireWire drive, and I have 100% confidence that I've restored my exact surround balance across six channels, with all the exact processing, effortlessly. And in surround, this is even more critical, because the relationship among six channels is even greater; the spec is even tighter to make your mix work. So I think mixing surround in the box is clearly the way to go for any kind of production where you're going to be expected to provide revisions—which, by the way, is everything!

We found Pro Tools to be essential. We use both SRS Circle Surround and, lately, more Dolby Pro Logic. We've done surround commercials that were on Monday Night Football, and a bunch that ran on Super Bowl Sunday, for advertisers like Chevy, Michelob, and McDonald's. In some cases we would do the surround mix, but in other cases it would be delivered to us for matrix encoding.

We had mixed a Chevy spot for Super Bowl Sunday, the client had approved it, and all was well. We had done it for an agency in Detroit, and we were in Chicago. On the Thursday before the Super Bowl, we were in New York at Avatar Studios, and we got a call in the afternoon from the agency in Detroit saying the network had rejected the edit, demanded a few changes of a few frames, and had a window of five hours to deliver the revised spot, and could we fix the soundtrack. We said, sure. We had them FTP us the new edit—we had their session file with us on a FireWire drive, as we travel with all our current projects with us. Because, with Pro Tools, we're not facility-bound anymore. We pulled up the project, made the editorial changes, walked across the street to Dolby and re-encoded it, and put the resulting edited mix back on their site. In an hour we had remixed it, in another hour we had it fully re-encoded, put it up on the site, and the client had it within three hours. They didn't even know we were in New York!

Q: How do you monitor your encoded surround signal?

A: For Dolby Pro Logic II, for example, we typically take our mix and monitor through the Dolby Pro Logic II encoder and decoder. We print the encoded mix back within our session file, and then monitor that through the decoder and again double-check it in surround, stereo, and mono. Then we deliver it as a two-channel Lt/Rt master, because that track—the output of the encoder—is the Lt/Rt. That's what we're delivering on our commercials.

Q: How have your clients and media agencies responded to surround commercial production?

A: Although we're pretty experienced with HD 5.1 broadcasting, having worked on the Grammys, etc., what we found when we went to talk to our advertising clients was a bit surprising: They were not yet particularly interested in the HD 5.1 transmission path. They felt that was a year away, when there would be a substantial enough audience for their clients to really recognize the value of that. But what they *were* very interested in was the audience that watches standard-definition television in surround. They have become aware that home theaters are very common and that families all over America, something like a third of them, have purchased home theaters. With that large number out there, it means that people could be listening to all the marquee events through their home theaters. We were able to show the advertisers that surround was a way that the programming is being delivered—on the Super Bowl, on the Grammys, the Oscars, but not just those shows. You can include all the prime-time programs like Fox Sports, NASCAR, the NBA, *West Wing, NYPD, ER*—all of this is delivered in surround.

Q: What format are they delivered in?

A: It's matrix-encoded surround. Some of it is in Dolby Pro Logic, some is in SRS Circle Surround. Either of the decoders, Circle Surround and Pro Logic II, will decode the other. So to the consumer, it's not particularly critical what they have. For the advertiser—and this is key—if somebody is listening to the program in surround (the standard-def broadcast), if the commercial mixed in stereo is now monitored through the surround decoders, the impact of the audio is diminished. It was then in their best interest to mix matrix-encoded surround.

Q: How does that then get to the consumer?

A: In standard-def broadcasting, it's effortless. It goes on the digi Beta master, goes to the stations, and it's broadcast. It's not even notated, because this is a transparent process to the broadcaster; its just a two-channel stereo mix. But if you decode it at your home, you will get an immersive surround effect from your decoder. The rear channels are stereo. Dolby Pro Logic, Pro Logic II, and Circle Surround put out six channels. The format called Dolby Surround was a four-channel system: It was L, C, R, and Surround. Dolby Pro Logic II is six channels, and is not bandwidth-limited in the rear channels, which it used to be. I don't consider it the equivalent of discrete, and if you're too radical in your panning when your target is matrix encoding, you'll get some cancellations in stereo and mono that you won't like. So you'll have to mix differently, which is our area of expertise with our clients, if your target is an Lt/Rt, as opposed to a discrete Dolby Digital broadcast. In commercials, I think we're about a year away from clients asking the agencies to supply dual masters: an HD 5.1 for that transmission path, and a standard-def matrix-encoded for that transmission path. They're not requesting it yet. Circle Surround is handled in the same way. We've used them both; Circle Surround has been an analog process. We've also gotten into the metadata of the Dolby process and we find that useful.

Q: What reverbs are you using in surround?

A: I'm using Pro Tools ReVibe and Trillium's Space. To have six-channel reverbs and dynamics, like Impact and Maxim and these reverbs, to have these parameters recallable, I can travel now with just my FireWire drive and my iLok, and I'm done. That's all I need to make sure I can provide the clients what they need.

Q: What other kinds of work do you produce in surround?

A: In addition to commercials, we've done the mixing for a number of music projects and DVDs: The Bonnaroo DVD, *270 Miles from Graceland*, Anthrax's *The Music of Mass Destruction*. I'm also working on a Street Racing DVD right now in surround. We also do DVD authoring, such as projects for the *Soundstage* TV show on PBS. We did the DVD for the two-hour Fleetwood Mac special for *Soundstage*, which has a surround track on it.

Grammy Awards for Surround Sound

Below is a portion of an article I wrote for Digidesign's DigiZine online magazine about the Grammys' new Best Surround Sound Album award category. It further reinforces the importance of surround production, regardless of the medium it's delivered on, and its overall impact.

Finally. After years of trying, we've got ourselves a new Grammy Award field. "Production, Surround Sound" was recently ratified by the Recording Academy, and the first category passed is for Best Surround Sound Album.

For those of you who thought surround sound was a fringe field, or weren't sure if you should get into it, this should be a clear sign of the future. It's exciting because Pro Tools is an incredibly powerful platform to mix surround on. All the tools you need are probably inside your computer already. If not, get the wheels turning!

Over the course of those years trying to get this award passed, it was often stated that we hoped the winners of the future were just learning to mix surround in their bedroom. Who knows who will win their own Surround Grammy Award? It certainly could be you.

However, like anything else truly worthwhile, it will take work. You'll have to put in the time to research how to mix surround, what technical aspects are involved, and how you work with five or more speakers instead of two—among many other things. Don't let it scare you, though—it's my opinion that if you can learn to use Pro Tools in stereo, you've already got the basics of surround mixing down. There are just a few more variables you'll have to consider.

Let's take a look at some of the particulars of the new Grammy Award.

To begin with, the award has no specific musical genre. It could be a classical surround mix, rock, pop, dance, or even polka. Also, all delivery mediums are included; it's for commercial releases on DVD-Video, DVD-Audio, or SA-CD that provide an original surround mix on the disc. The award will go to the surround remix engineer, surround producer (if any), and surround mastering engineer (if any).

Here a few quotes right from the proposal itself, to help give you some more insight into the award:

"Eligible entries must be commercially released on DVD-Video, DVD-Audio, or SA-CD. Eligible entries must provide an original surround mix (not electronically re-purposed) of four or more channels. Eligible entries must meet all other Grammy Awards eligibility requirements.

"Since these awards recognize creative achievement, evaluations should be 'format agnostic,' so that all multichannel surround release formats would be viewed equally. These Grammy Award categories are intended to recognize audio expertise and creativity, so any included video content should not be considered."

A special nominating committee (since it's a craft award) will select five final nominations, and the final award will be given out at the Grammy ceremony. Record labels that are registered with NARAS, as well as individual members, may enter.

Surround sound mixing is an art form, deserving of an award such as a Grammy. While this is the first award of its kind, hopefully the future will broaden the scope to cover additional surround fields. Just think about how much material is coming out in surround these days: movies, concert videos, new and classic records, HDTV and standard-def television broadcasts—and, of course, lots of video games.

Special thanks go to the other committee members who helped get this award passed. If you see any of them around, let them know you're mixing surround or at least learning how! Thanks to: Phil Ramone, Al Schmitt, Hank Neuberger, Howard Massey, Elliot Scheiner, George Massenberg, Frank Fillipetti, Bob Ludwig, Tony Visconti, Eric Shilling, Jeff Levison, Rory Kaplan, Paul Stubblebine, and to Leslie Lewis and the entire Recording Academy.

Follow the DVD

Follow the DVD

On the enclosed DVD, I have included over a dozen 5.1 audio examples in the Dolby Digital AC-3 format. Simply set your surround receiver for Dolby Digital and follow along with the text.

The "Audio Examples" section features eleven various short clips and the "Full Mixes" portion features three complete mixes. Written descriptions for all examples are included below: (Note that the menu music itself is in stereo, in order to accentuate the 5.1 examples).

Example 1: Vocal Center Channel 0% Center

Here is an example of placing a vocal in the Center channel only, with the Center % on the Digidesign panner set to 0. This creates a truly "phantom" center, where the Left and Right Front speakers carry the image. There is no audio coming out of the Center channel.

Example 2: Vocal Center Channel 100% Center

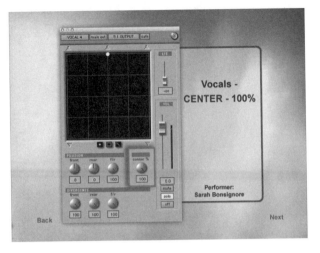

This is the same vocal as the previous example, but the Center percentage on the panner is set to 100%. Now the vocal comes out of the Center channel only, with no bleed into the Left and Right Front channels at all. This can be dangerous in a real-world mix, as the consumer may not have a center channel or may have an incorrect setup.

Example 3: Vocal Center Channel, 50%, into Waves R360 Reverb

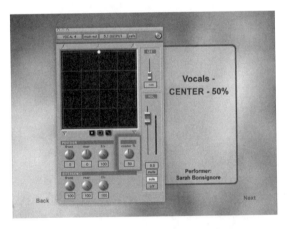

By setting the Center % 50, you would then have an even mix of vocal in the Left Front, Center, and Right Front channels. By adding a send to the Waves R360 Reverb, the overall effect becomes warm and round—from just a single channel of vocals.

Example 4: Four Channels of Vocals—Dry—50% Center

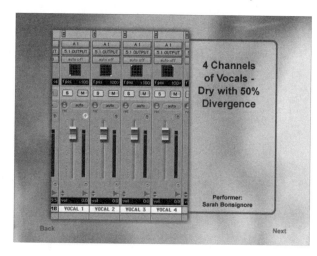

Here is an example of using four channels of vocals, all recorded by the same singer, to thicken up a surround mix. Although you could simply duplicate a single track four times, having the singer overdub themselves instead, creates a thick, natural chorusing. Each take is then panned into the four corners of the mix: Front Left (FL), Front Right (FR), Left Surround (Ls), and Right Surround (Rs). With the 50% Center send on the front Left and Right tracks, the Center channel will at least have some information in it, although this method is intended to use with backgrounds.

Example 5: Four Channels of Vocals into Waves R360 Reverb

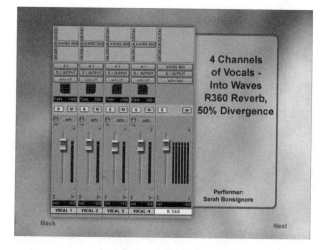

This is the same example as previous, but with the inclusion of a surround reverb, the Waves R360. As you can hear, it creates a lush, ambient, and even sound. Note that the R360 has only reverb tails, and no pre-delay or early reflections. Using four vocals, you could send either a small amount from each one (which I have done in this example), or a bit more each from the front or rear tracks. An alternate method, should you not have access to a surround reverb, is to use two stereo reverbs, panned to the front and rear accordingly. If you make the RT (Reverb Time) a bit longer on the rear reverb, you have a naturally decaying space. Conversely, you could also use four mono reverbs for a totally different effect.

Example 6: Alto Sax with Waves 360 Imager Bypassed

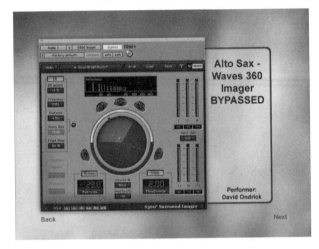

This is an alto sax, recorded in a carpeted hallway with an Audio Technica 4060 mic and a Focusrite preamp. The Waves 360 Imager is used instead of a Digidesign panner. In this example, it is bypassed, revealing the natural sound of the sax in a hallway. It is panned into the Left Front speaker with the Center percentage set to 50%.

Example 7: Alto Sax into Waves 360 Imager

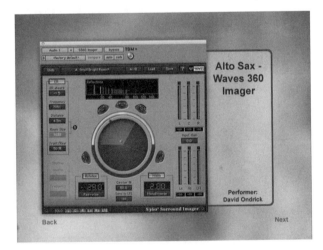

The sax is now placed inside a virtual room with the S360 Imager. The distance is set to 4.5m and the early reflections are quite present. There is no send to the LFE, and the Front/Rear percentage is set to 50%, providing a nice, even sound through-out. Using a 360 Imager is very useful for making a track—even if it's recorded dry—stand out in a mix.

Example 8: Istanbul 20-inch Ping Cymbal, Centered in the Panner

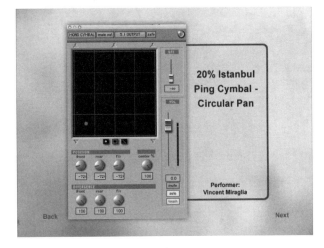

This is a single stroke hit of an Instanbul 20-inch Ping cymbal, recorded close with an Earthworks QTC-1 omni microphone and an Earthworks preamp. By panning it in the middle of a Digidesign panner, an equal amount of surround energy will appear in all five speakers. In a mix, though, with all the other instruments, this may get lost a bit. However, it does show how you can create an equally balanced sound with a single channel.

Example 9: Istanbul 20-inch Ping Cymbal, Reversed, Circular Pan

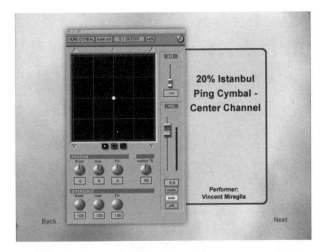

This is the same cymbal as previous, but reversed in Pro Tools, and panned in a circular motion. This pan was done with a mouse, so it is not completely balanced, but that's why I wanted you to hear it as such. It still works to create an almost dizzying effect. The Center percentage was left at 100%, so the signal strength is full when it passes by that speaker. Be careful with overusing circular pans in a surround mix—only do it when absolutely necessary. It is cool, though!

Example 10: Drums/Percussion Full Surround Mix

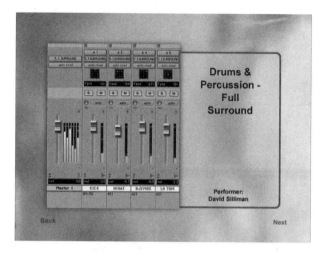

This is an example of using a surround miking technique on a full drum/percussion kit. Aside from the traditional microphones on the kick, hi-hats, djembe, a setup of four B&K microphones were placed around the kit in the live room at Clubhouse Studios. There is a pair of 4007 cardioids in front, about eight feet apart and five feet from the kit, and 4011 omnis behind the kit in the exact same configuration. The drum fills were recorded with the same configuration, only using Earthworks QTC-1s and TC-30ks. Listen to the Romeros Un Segundo Una Vida example to hear this technique used in a full mix.

Example 11: Romero's "Un Segundo Una Vida"

Song: "Un Segundo Una Vida"

"Un Segundo Una Vida" was recorded in discrete multichannel from the project's inception. Captured at Bear Tracks Studios in Suffern, New York and Clubhouse Studios in Rhinebeck, New York, we tried to take advantage of the beautiful natural acoustics provided by each space. The signal path was fed directly out of the microphones into a Sony DMX-R100 console and straight to high resolution Pro Tools. Microphones used included Earthworks TC-30Ks and QTC-1s, Sony C-800Gs, DPA 4011 and 4009s and several Neumanns. Additional preamps included Earthworks, Groove Tube, Focusrite, and Aphex.

Percussionist David Silliman's "world kit," placed in the middle of the Clubhouse's live room, was miked in a traditional fashion—with the addition of four B&K microphones in a quad setup around him, cardioids in front, about eight feet apart and five feet from the kit, and omnis behind him in the exact same configuration. Recording this way allows for incredible spaciousness in the mix, as well as providing real, natural reverb. We also created a separate four-channel overdub for drum fills (using that same mic setup), since there are plenty of tracks when recording direct to Pro Tools.

The strings, consisting of Andy Munitz on violin and viola and his brother Charles Munitz on cello, were recorded piece by piece. Overdubbing each string part four times, we created our own "section." But since strings are usually miked up at more of a distance (and as a whole section), I needed a more ambient overall sound. To accomplish this, I created a string submix, and sent it out to two Hot House monitors in the studio's spacious live room. Two Earthworks QTC-1 omni mics were placed in front of each speaker, about four feet back, and two Earthworks TC-30ks were positioned about eight feet high in the back far corners of the room. This "re-record," combined with the direct tracks and some Concertgebouw Impulse Response reverb, creates a warm, sweet string sound from just two players. It's a good example of "work with what you've got" in surround.

The guitars were recorded in stereo, using the Earthworks QTC-1s and Focusrite preamps. They are panned either hard left or right, with the second microphone in the 2 o'clock or 10 o'clock position across the front. Aside from a small amount of direct send to the rear Left and Right surrounds, I also used Concertgebouw reverb on them from the Sony S-777. The bass was recorded direct into an Aguilar preamp, with one channel straight and one channel of effects. The project was mixed all inside Pro Tools at Gizmo in New York City.

Example 12: Romero's Live at Trinity Church, New York

Song: "El Reynado"

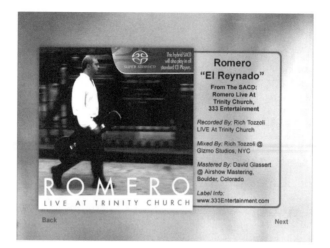

Romero's *Live at Trinity Church*, New York, was just that—a live recording in a beautiful acoustic environment. This church, dating back to the mid-1800s, is a pristine place to make a recording. The band, consisting of Romero on guitar, Mario Rodriguez on bass, Oscar Feldman on sax, and Gilad on percussion, set up on the pulpit at the front of the church.

What many people don't know is that there is a fully functional Pro Tools studio tie-lined into that pulpit! It sits upstairs, and each instrument was close-miked and fed to high-quality preamps on the side of the "stage." Those signals were then fed upstairs, and captured into Pro Tools and a set of Alesis M-20 recorders. I set up two Earthworks TC-30ks about 20 feet apart and 10 feet from the stage to capture the essence of the church itself.

This is a great example of using natural acoustics in a surround recording, as you can hear certain percussion hits reflect off the side and back walls. There were no overdubs, and this is truly a live concert recording. The two "split-omni" Earthworks microphones were also used as the reverb on the stereo mix.

Example 13: Larry Chernicoff's October

Song: "Windhorse"

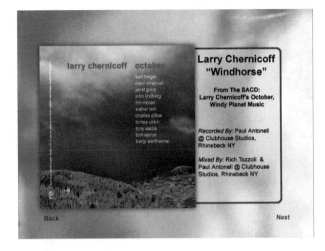

Windhorse was recorded and mixed at the Clubhouse studios in Rhinebeck, New York. Engineer and studio owner Paul Antonell captured the ensemble with surround in mind from the beginning, and we mixed it from the conductor's perspective. I thought it best to have the artist, Larry Chernicoff, describe the feeling of producing surround music from an artist point of view.

Notes from Larry Chernicoff:

The first time a musician hears surround sound, its spaciousness, clarity, and fidelity, it takes about eight seconds to understand that you have to plan all your sessions for the rest of your life in a new way. So when it came time to record, it was clear in my head. Karl Berger conducted the group in the studio, standing in front of the players, who were laid out in a semicircle in front of him. Rather than the usual "player's perspective" or "audience perspective" discussion, we knew what we wanted from the beginning: conductor's perspective. We laid out the surround field so that the listener is sitting right in front of Karl's music stand.

"Windhorse" was written specifically for this group, which can be thought of as either a large chamber ensemble or a miniature orchestra. The very first time I went to check out the studio (many months before the recording) I brought with me a little chart of how I wanted the musicians to sit in the room—the string trio off to the left, the four winds arrayed from center (lower-pitched instruments) out to the right (higher-pitched instruments), percussion in the center rear, piano and vibes down the middle, etc. I had it all laid out in my mind.

My concept in this music was to achieve a chamber music sound with the dynamic and improvisational feel of jazz. So we went for for a live, unplugged, organic, acoustic sound, using real instruments, minimal percussion, and no electronics at all.

Because we planned a hybrid SACD, we had to do two separate mixes. Starting with the stereo mix helped us get familiar with everything we had tracked, and do some edits in Pro Tools. I had the finished stereo mix in my car for a few weeks before we came back to do the surround mix, and I thought I knew the music really, really well. But the playback through the 5.1 system was an amazing experience from the very first minute. There were things in the music which I, as the composer, had never even heard during the stereo mixing process—little phrases in Tim Moran's soprano sax solo, the overtones in the blend of wind instruments, the fantastic live bass sound that Paul captured. It was truly amazing. Everyone in the studio was pretty blown away by the raw material we had to work with in each track. We remained true to the original concept we had come up with more than a year before the mixing session, and pretty much laid it all out from conductor's perspective. Once we had everything dialed in, we stayed pretty close to that layout for all the tracks.

The title of this piece, "Windhorse," is a translation of the Tibetan term "Lung Ta," which is a flag printed with prayers, believed to send blessings out into the world as it blows in the wind. You often see them in photos of Himalayan mountain passes and Tibetan monasteries. I wrote this piece in 2002, hoping to capture some of that spirit.

Additional Resources

Here are several books, websites, and a magazine and DVD that I highly recommend:

Surround Professional Magazine
> www.surroundpro.com

How to Set Up Your Surround Studio (DVD)
> by Bobby Owsinski
> EuroJam International/United Entertainment Media

> The complete guide to choosing, placing, and calibrating the equipment needed in setting up your surround studio

The Mixing Engineer's Handbook
> by Bobby Owsinski
> ArtistPro Books/Hal Leonard Publishing
> www.artistpro.com

> Features a section dedicated to general surround mixing techniques and philosophies

The Mastering Engineer's Handbook
> by Bobby Owsinski
> ArtistPro Books/Hal Leonard Publishing
> www.artistpro.com

> Features a section dedicated to general surround mastering techniques as well as DVD and SACD delivery

The Recording Engineer's Handbook

by Bobby Owsinski

ArtistPro Books/Hal Leonard Publishing

www.artistpro.com

Features a section dedicated to general surround mics and miking techniques and philosophies

5.1 Up and Running

by Tomlinson Holman

Examines topics such as loudspeakers, acoustics, bass management, recording techniques, tips for postproduction, and much more.

Surround Associates

www.surroundassociates.com

Surround sound FAQ, glossary, various articles on surround miking, asset preparation, and surround sound delivery

Recommendations for Surround Sound Production

www.grammy.com/pe_wing/guidelines/index.aspx

A useful document from the NARAS Producers & Engineers Wing covering many aspects of surround sound production, setup and delivery.

Index

Vocals
    in Center channel, 147–48
    four channels of, 148–49
Volkman, John, 1
VTR, layback to, 87

W
Warnerphonic, 2
Waves 360, 12–13, 14, 37–40, 97–101, 148,
    149–50
Waves IR-1, 102–3
WMA 9 (Windows Media Audio 9), 120–21

X
X/Y Grid, 35

Y
Yamaha DM2000, 59
Yamaha O2R96, 59
Yamaha SREV1, 115

Z
Zuckerman, Steve, 136